bone biographer's casebook

It takes exacting reporting and recording skill, shared dedicated goals,
a broad range of skeletal and dental data and exceptional teamwork to
have the power to bring a bag of bones back to life again.

Published by LeanTo Press
A Division of infoBits®LLC
4712 15th Avenue South
Minneapolis, MN 55417, USA

ART DIRECTOR: Katherine Meyers
EDITOR AND WRITER: Miriam Rothstein
COVER AND INTERIOR DESIGN: Katherine Meyers
PRODUCTION COORDINATOR: Katherine Meyers

Written in Bone: Bone Biographer's Casebook
©2009 Douglas W. Owsley
©2009 LeanTo Press

The credits on pages 139 constitute an extension of this copyright page.

First Edition: January 2009

Library of Congress Cataloging-in-Publication Data

Written in Bone: Bone Biographer's Casebook: Owsley, Bruwelheide

ISBN 978-0-615-23346-8

1. Science-Forensic Anthropology, Archaeology, Crime Scene Investigation, Anatomy, Medicine.
2. History-American, African American, Civil War, World War II
3. Art-Design, Photography

Written in Bone: Bone Biographer's Casebook. Printed in Saint Paul, Minnesota, USA, by Impressive Print Inc. www.impressiveprint.com

COVER IMAGE: Ectocranial view of occipital bone showing thinning and formation of holes. "Hair-on-end" appearance of infant cranium with rickets, Lead Coffin Burial #3 Historic St. Mary's City, ca. 1683. Photograph by Brittney Tatchell, Smithsonian Institution.

CONTENTS

ACKNOWLEDGEMENTS

First and foremost we thank Chip Clark, whose extraordinary talents in photography elevate our ability to document and interpret the evidence and stories in bone. Next, we thank and acknowledge the vision and efforts of Kate Meyers and Miriam Rothstein whose amazing talents and perseverance helped craft this manuscript.

Our thanks to our families: Doug's wife Susanne and daughters Hilary and Kimberly, and father Bill Owsley; Kari's husband Kurt, daughter Beret, son Calvin, and parents Marv and Becky Sandness. Your support has allowed us to meet demanding and unpredictable schedules. For your love and guidance we are eternally grateful.

STAFF AND VOLUNTEERS
Heartfelt and special thanks to our staff and volunteers who keep the office running and work in the field: Dale Brown, Bill Hanna, John Imlay, Vicki Simon, Sandra Schlachtmeyer, Cass Taylor, Aleithea Williams, Dana Kollmann; special remembrance to dear friend and colleague, Malcolm "Rich" Richardson, whose years of dedicated service on behalf of cemetery preservation and burial investigation proved invaluable in the investigation of historic sites in Virginia and Maryland.

Archaeological colleagues: Henry Miller, Tim Riordan, and Silas Hurry of Historic St. Mary's City; Bill Kelso, Bly Straube, Jamie May, Michael Lavin, and Danny Schmidt of APVA Preservation Virginia/ Historic Jamestowne; Nick Luccketti, Garret Fesler, and Tonia Rock of The James River Institute for Archaeology; Alain Outlaw and Merry Outlaw of Archaeological & Cultural Solutions, Inc.; and Al Luckenbach and Jane Cox of Anne Arundel County's Lost Towns Project.

Colleagues who offered support and expertise: Dan Rogers, Dave Hunt, Laurie Burgess, Bruno Frohlich, Dept. of Anthropology, NMNH; Lee Jantz, University of Tennessee; Ashley McKeown, University of Montana; and Kate Spradley, University of Texas, San Marcos.

We humbly thank our teachers and mentors whose passion and commitment to the field was our inspiration: Bill Bass, George Gill, Dale Henning, Richard Jantz, and Karl Reinhard.

Thank you to the staff of the National Museum of Natural History: Cristián Samper/Director; Hans-Dieter Sues/Associate Director of Research and Collections; Elizabeth Duggal/ Public Programs; Christine Elias and Jennifer Williams/Development; Rena Selim, Barbara Stauffer, Siobhan Starrs, Michael Lawrence/ Exhibits; *and to our generous donors and sponsors who helped make the Written in Bone exhibition a reality.*

To most people, the human skeleton is death personified, a stark reminder of the transient nature of our physical existence. To trained eyes, however, these bones also provide a rich record of changes both subtle and gross, reflecting good times and bad in an individual's life. Not only does the skeleton reveal gender, age, and ethnicity, but diet, disease, toil, and violence all leave telltale marks. Sophisticated new methods for studying bones continue to reveal new kinds of data. Each skeleton tells the life story of an individual human being.

At the Smithsonian's National Museum of Natural History, renowned forensic anthropologists Douglas Owsley and Karin Bruwelheide have worked tirelessly to unlock the secrets of the dead and interpret them for the living. They have illuminated the lives of early Europeans and Africans in America 400 years ago. Regardless of their social status, they led lives of toil and hardship, and their bones provide a stark record of struggle and endurance. Douglas and Karin's research on this subject will be profiled in the exhibit *Written in Bone: Forensic Files of the 17th-Century Chesapeake* at the National Museum of Natural History.

Homo homini lupus est - man is a wolf to man. Throughout human history, countless men, women, and children have met untimely, unnatural deaths. Douglas and Karin have exhumed and studied soldiers from America's greatest domestic tragedy, the Civil War, as well as victims of atrocities in foreign countries. They have assisted law enforcement in identifying and establishing the cause of death for many who have been murdered and mutilated. Their forensic work has frequently helped bring the perpetrators of such outrages to justice and provided a measure of closure to the victims' families and friends. Douglas and Karin never forget that the skeletal remains on their examination table were once living human beings, and empathy is as much part of their work as is scientific knowledge.

This volume collects some of the skeleton stories that Douglas and Karin have recorded over the years. I invite you to follow the efforts of these two master sleuths as they bring the dead back to life. Scientific photographer Chip Clark has long worked with Douglas and Karin in documenting their cases. A selection of previously unpublished images from his portfolio now vividly illustrates this book.

Hans-Dieter Sues, PhD
Associate Director for Research and Collections
National Museum of Natural History
Smithsonian Institution

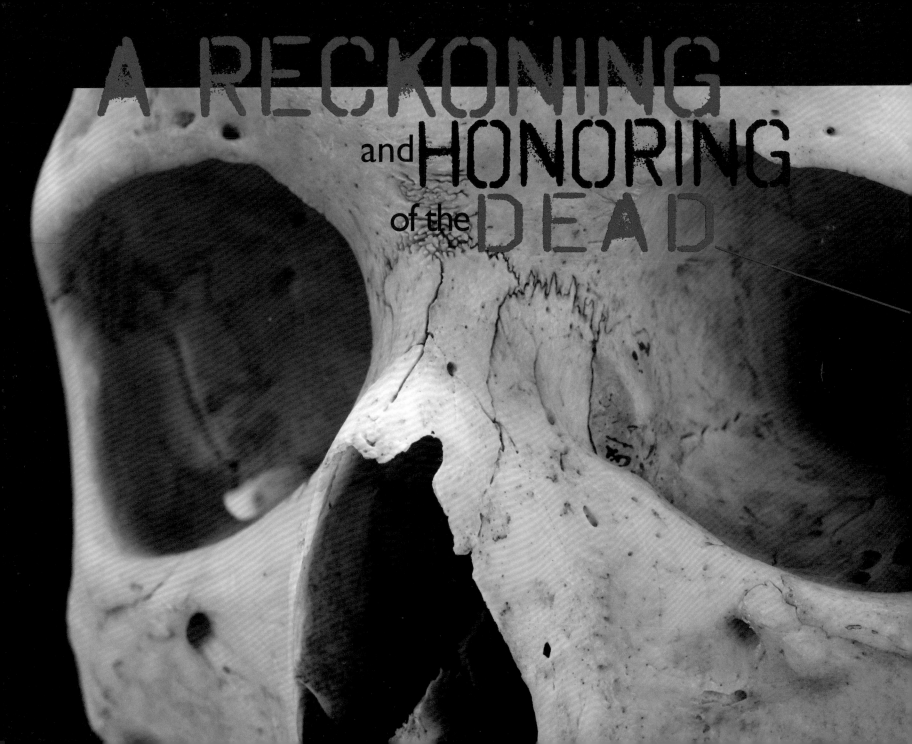

A RECKONING
and HONORING
of the DEAD

When Douglas Owsley and Karin Bruwelheide entered the field, they didn't know that it would lead them to create the exhibition, *Written in Bone: Forensic Files of the 17th-Century Chesapeake*. In this business you don't choose your subjects. They choose you.

It may take decades and, yes, luck to amass enough data on a given human population to be in a position to make any generalizations—let alone to curate an exhibition with the significance of *Written in Bone*. The earth does not give up its dead in an orderly manner or with any consistency. At the Smithsonian, you get a call, you answer it. As Owsley puts it, "Our work is very opportunistic."

WRITTEN IN BONE: BONE BIOGRAPHER'S CASEBOOK is an intimate glimpse into the lives of ordinary people in extraordinary circumstances. We witness calm and focused attention being brought to impossible situations, under conditions that cut against the grain. We experience what it means to give the least powerful a voice in the thrill of returning a name to its proper owner. We see the compassionate hand of service and care extended to both the living and dead. Bruwelheide feels responsible for giving the bones of the dead, the most disenfranchised of all, a chance to speak. She is known best for her outstanding osteological skills, but when she looks into a box of bones, she sees an individual identity, a name, a face. Her goal: let's think about this and try to place it in a context. Bruwelheide is determined to fill in the human story, not any story, but your story, she wants not only to give you a name—but a voice.

Physical Anthropologists are known for their exhaustive methodologies, not for their philosophical musings. Like field notes of site excavations, bioarchaeologists have extensively used their photographic archives for reference. For every individual skeleton restored from commingled remains, for every individual named and unnamed, hundreds and hundreds of scientific photographs are taken from every conceivable point of view.

If we could sum up Owsley and Bruwelheide's philosophy of life, it would be, "Everything matters, nothing is insignificant." Scientists first, they are attracted by the questions. As anthropologists they accept what is given—the facts, the indignities, the shock. For a scientist, it's all about the mystery to be solved. The driving force is not in the existential reality, but in putting the pieces together again.

At the end of a long day of looking through ring binders with images of genocidal madness and ordinary murder, Owsley confessed, with the kind of resignation one might expect after a long interrogation, that what he wanted was to be able to show that all the work they do is worth it. Silence is best, you come to think, respectful silence.

If there is a solution to the problem of evil, it must be a philosophy of life. Surely, what these photographs reveal of Owsley and Bruwelheide's work is in the direction of a solution, a corrective turn, a kind of restitution.

Owsley and Bruwelheide's office.

They have traveled between academic research and public service. They have trained students, conducted scientific inquiries, collected data, and published articles. They have acted as consultants to the medico-legal community and used their scientific and investigative skills to serve the broader community. This book is a novel effort to create a lasting testimony to the value of the work and methodology of the most fact-obsessed people in all of anthropology—the forensic anthropologist.

Let the bones speak for themselves.

Kate Meyers
Miriam Rothstein

BC #: 5351

Accession #(s):
1998.026.001: Excavations at Patuxent Point

THE HUMAN
BODY IS NOT
THE WORLD

Site #(s)/Lot #(s):
18CV271 (277)
Grave #10: 2107 E

AND
YET IT IS

Contents:
Human Remains

-CHARLES WRIGHT

Room	Range	Bank	Shelf
CS	**H3**	**1**	**7**

10

Human Remains...

The phrase is so evocative.
As if these dead— forgotten,
missing and unnamed,
would never Rest in Peace
until we understood their cry
from the deep time of Being Human.

" " Unless we know who we were,
                we can't know who we are.

There's nothing in the archaeological record that can tell you more than the skeleton. Nearly every interaction with our social and physical environment—what we ate, how much we carried, how tightly we were swaddled, how roughly we were treated—ends up being recorded in our bones.

The visual and data archive we create is a way of preserving a site once it has been excavated. The archive gives researchers and students the option of going back to address lingering questions and the opportunity to ask and answer new ones. WRITTEN IN BONE: BONE BIOGRAPHER'S CASEBOOK offers a perspective on the science that made this visual and written record possible.

Photographs are an integral part of anthropological records, and photo documentation can consist of thousands of images. As forensic anthropologists, we depend on these images to describe, analyze, interpret, and communicate the story of human remains.

As scientists, our goal is to develop extensive databases and to build representative sample sizes. We use these databases to document and interpret past events, and for tracking health-related or secular trends through time. In these ways, we increase our undertanding of archaeological and historical records.

Contemporary forensic work is possible in its current form because scientists have developed these extensive databases. By studying a great diversity of human skeletons of known age, sex, and ethnic background, we can develop a comparative basis for evaluating contemporary human identification (forensic) cases.

Through premier archaeological investigations at Historic St. Mary's City in Maryland and Jamestown, Virginia, we are fortunate to have read hundreds of the most personal individual accounts ever recorded from the early-17th-century colonial period. Historians of 17th-century America have a limited number of documents from which to learn.

It has taken a lifetime of work to collect meaningful samples. From 17th-century Chesapeake sites alone, 300 individuals have been identified and studied. This fraction of the number of colonists who came to this region provides a foundation for expanded research.

In order to compile comprehensive data, we meticulously record hundreds of observations and measurements for each skeleton. We're seeking to tell as much of their individual story as possible—age, sex, ancestry, stature, activities, habits and health, diet and, perhaps, even the cause of their death.

The Smithsonian's National Museum of Natural History is responsible for curating human skeletal remains from around the world. The physical anthropology collection is irreplaceable. It represents 30,000 individuals extensively studied by biological anthropologists and health scientists.

In looking at many skeletons, our goal is to understand the story of a group of people. The human experience through time and space as told by those who lived it– that's what we strive for. Each set of remains contributes to our understanding of ourselves and our place in the world. Tremendous advances in analytical capability and access to reference collections from different time periods, environments, and cultures make it possible to seek answers to questions that were beyond our research only a few decades ago.

We are not only advocates for those whose lives previously went unrecorded, we are advocates for the next generation of teachers and researchers.

Training in forensic anthropology, osteology, and skeletal pathology is dependent upon broad experience gained by looking at the bones of many individuals– prehistoric, historic and modern. Knowledge of the skeleton is experience-based and must be continuously accumulated and refined. In order to recognize abnormal or pathological conditions, a student must first have knowledge of normal variation among individuals.

As Smithsonian-based researchers, teachers, and consultants, our purpose and our efforts lead to a deeper understanding of the individuals whose lives, in a sense, we are able to bring to life. We are responsible to the public to preserve this aspect of our collective heritage and to train present and future generations in interpreting this unique "body" of evidence. Separated from its scientific context and interpretation, an image of a skull is lifeless no matter how artistic we judge it to be. Separated from their story, human remains are lost to history. "

THE FATE OF BONES

" The skeleton is a personal legacy. It is an individual's life story—a gift to the present. "

-DOUGLAS OWSLEY

{ to the memory of Col. JOSEPH BRIDGER }

The Joseph Bridger Project

The Bridger Family Association was crucial to the excavation of the skeletal remains of Colonel Joseph Bridger (d.15 April 1686). The remains were exhumed from a small crypt beneath the ledger stone set in the floor of Saint Luke's Church, Smithfield, Virginia, the oldest standing English Church in America.

Douglas Owsley and Jean Birdsong Tomes look into a small crypt beneath the ledger stone inset of her ancestor Colonel Joseph Bridger Saint Luke's Church, Smithfield, Virginia.

Student intern Brittney Tatchell spent hours beneath the floor of St. Luke's Church in Smithfield, Virginia, working to excavate the crypt underneath the ledger stone set in the floor.

SACRED
To y MEMORY OF
HE HON.ble JOSEPH BRIDGER
Esq. COUNCEL OF STATE IN VIRG
NG TO KING CHARLES y 2d
ED APRIL y J5 : A.D. J686
WIFE 3 SONS & 4 DAUGHT

Nature silent mourn & can dumb
true worth to future Ages k
exprefsion Marble fure will
e best y ever on his gra
y late great M
al virtue
his

Douglas Owsley and Genevieve Turner Frost, in her 80s, looking into the crypt of her ancestor.

Greg Culler, a machinist at the Smithsonian, opens an 1864 Raymond cast iron coffin, October 23, 2006.

A Protocol for the Analysis of Cast-Iron Coffin Burials (Owsley and Bruwelheide)

1 PRELIMINARY STEPS describe and measure the coffin;

visual documentation (photographs)

describe the coffin opening and interior;

visual documentation of coffin, body, clothing (photography)

collect bacterial and mold samples from inside the coffin.

2 TAPHONOMIC OBSERVATIONS describe the body's condition document

preservation and postmortem alterations.

3 COMPUTED TOMOGRAPHY

create digital images of the body and artifacts

4 CLOTHING ANALYSIS work with historic costume expert to document and

interpret burial clothing, **photograph selected items...**

A COFFIN IS A SMALL DOMAIN

After two years of historical, forensic, and genealogical research, and DNA testing, a 15 year old boy was identified as William Taylor White of Accomack County, Virginia. He died after a short illness at Columbian College on January 24, 1852.

YET ABLE
TO CONTAIN
A CITIZEN OF
PARADISE
IN ITS
DIMINISHED
PLANE
—EMILY DICKINSON

X-ray: lead coffin of
Anne Wolseley Calvert

In 1992, archaeologists at Historic St. Mary's City, Maryland, opened a narrow, lead-covered, 17th-century wooden coffin to find well-preserved remains of a woman strewn with rosemary sprigs.

25

AND WHO SHALL SEPARATE THE DUST

WHAT LATER WE SHALL BE:

WHOSE KEEN DISCERNING EYE WILL

SCAN AND SOLVE THE MYSTERY?

-GEORGIA DOUGLAS JOHNSON

Crypt and remains of thirteen individuals, eleven of whom were Spanish diplomats, including emissary Ramón Power y Giralt, Puerto Rico's representative to the 1812 Spanish Constitutional Court.

Cádiz, Spain 2005, Martha Kate Spradley,
doctoral student working with Dr. Owsley,
cleans the fragments as they are being removed
and sorted into individuals.

Cádiz, Spain, 2005 Maria Perez Sanjurjo,
brushing the bones, student of Professor
Maria Cashion, Archaeologist and Physical
Anthropologist in Puerto Rico.

The essence of a good osteologist is the ability to detect what is going on in a skeleton, and then to utilize the right specialists and analytical methods to tease out and recover the story.

Karin Bruwelheide carefully studies the pathology of the dentition, noting teeth lost in life, the presence of cavities, abscesses, and periodontal disease.

THE MEASURE OF THINGS

"We haven't yet begun to tap the potential of these old bones.
-DOUGLAS OWSLEY

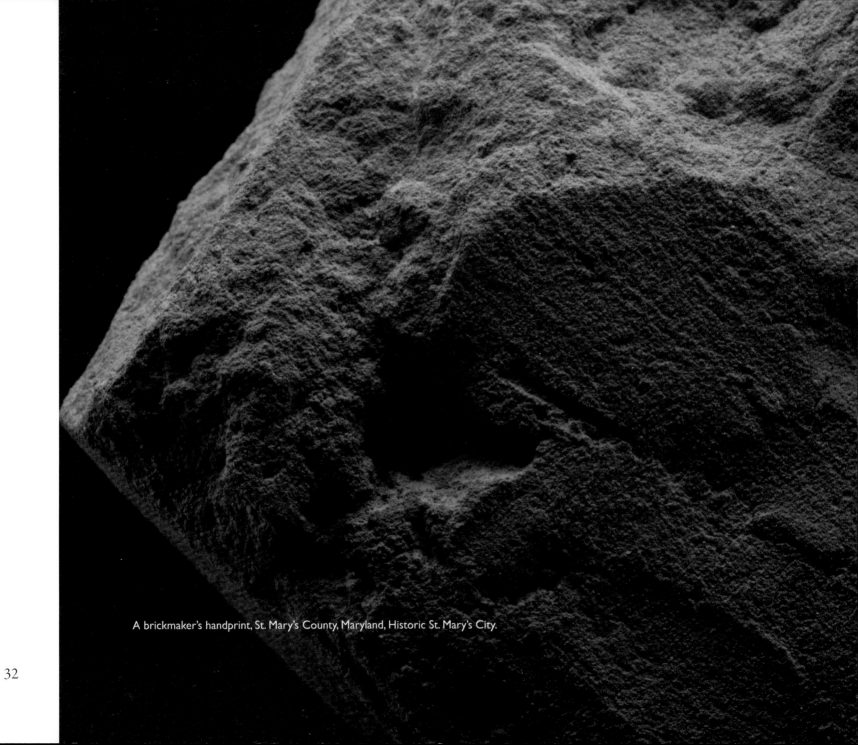

A brickmaker's handprint, St. Mary's County, Maryland, Historic St. Mary's City.

Jamestown Double Burials: Smithsonian forensic anthropologist Douglas Owsley and archaeologist William Kelso discuss the 1607 James Fort burial. APVA Preservation Virginia / Historic Jamestowne

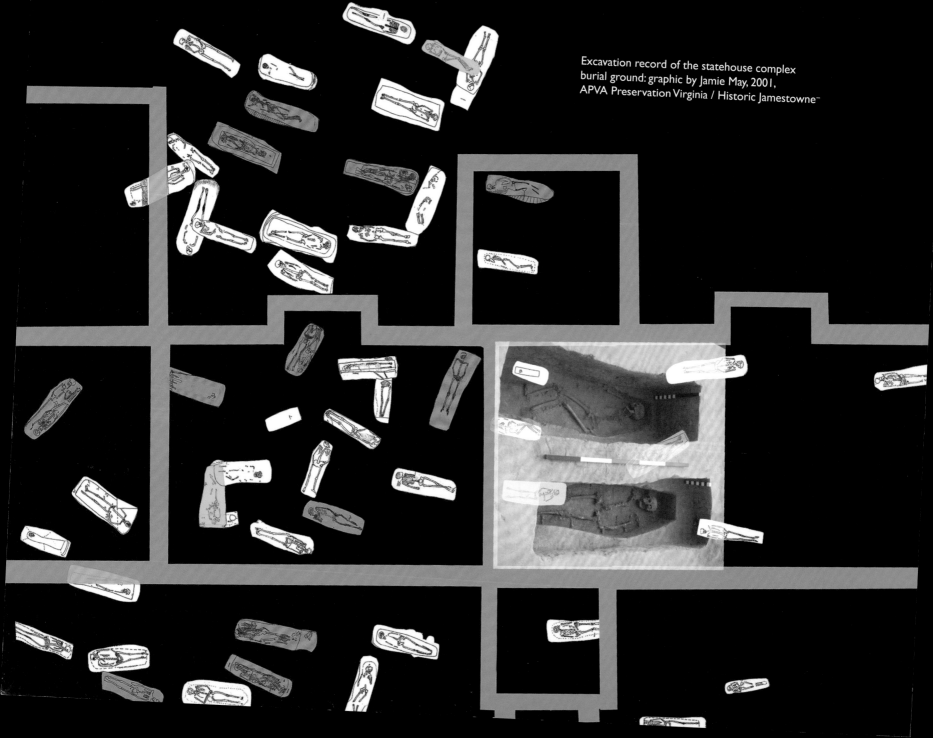

Excavation record of the statehouse complex
burial ground: graphic by Jamie May, 2001,
APVA Preservation Virginia / Historic Jamestowne™

Double Burial, James Fort, Virginia, 1607

The Statehouse Complex Burial
Map at James Fort, Virginia

Multiple Burials in Shaft

Burials with Clothing

Burials with Evidence of
Traumatic Death

Building Foundations
Overlay Burial Ground

A Breakdown in Burial Customs

The standard English practice in
the early 1600s was to bury the
dead without clothing, wrapped in a
winding-sheet or shroud. Most were
placed without a coffin in a carefully
dug shaft large enough to fit a body
extended on its back.

The statehouse cemetery holds a
mix of traditional and haphazard
burials. In some graves, the bodies
were face down, on their sides, or
bent to fit too small a grave shaft.
The unusually high death rate of
young adults in the statehouse
cemetery reflects both the crisis in
the community and the makeup of
the population of early Jamestown.
The remains are mostly male—
teenagers and young men.

Written in Bone Exhibit Script

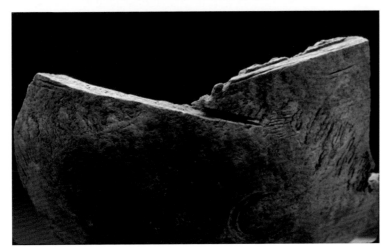

Cranial fragment of a European adult male, showing evidence of severe head injury. The circular cuts show an aborted surgical procedure called trephination. Additional cuts in the bone indicate an autopsy was also performed. James Fort site, ca.1607–1610, Jamestown, VA, APVA, Preservation Virginia / Historic Jamestowne.

The patient had suffered mortal blows to the head.

Trepanning saw, head and shank ca.1607–1630, James Fort site,
Jamestown, Virginia, APVA Preservation Virginia / Historic Jamestowne

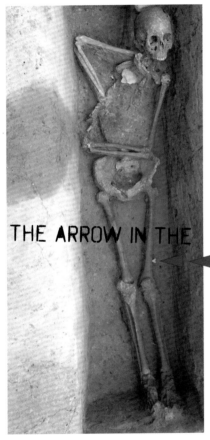

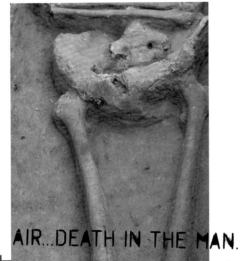

THE ARROW IN THE AIR...DEATH IN THE MAN.

AS SOMETHING FIRST PERCEIVED BY ACCIDENT

-CHRISTOPHER LOGUE

Skeletal remains of one of the first settlers of Jamestown, a young boy with an arrow point lodged in his leg.

He was one of the 104 men and boys who came to Virginia on the first ships in 1607.

A QUICK DEATH

might have been a

BLESSING

One of his front incisors was broken exposing the tooth's pulp chamber. New bone could be seen forming as his body tried to stem what must have been a raging infection. You can see the gaping hole in his jaw where a large abscess had formed. The poor boy would have soon died, even if the arrow hadn't found him.

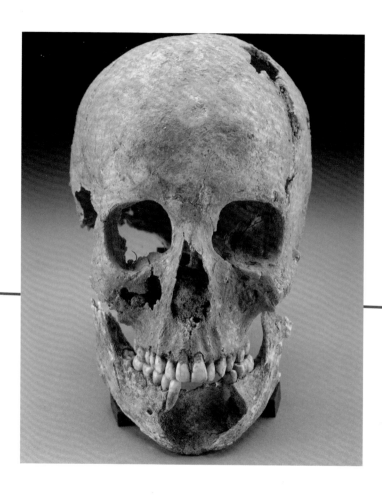

facial reconstruction
a combination of **ART & SCIENCE**

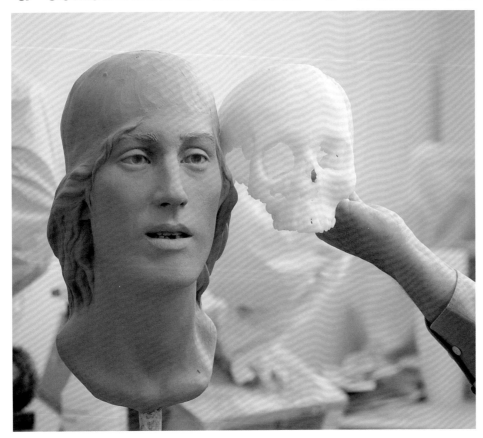

Sculpted bust by StudioEIS

JAMES FORT BOY/JAMESTOWN, VIRGINIA

a tangible impression of
real individuals FROM THE PAST.

This three-dimensional reconstruction of the James Fort Boy was created from a cast of his cranial remains. The features were systematically sculpted with modeling clay and other materials. The position and general shape of the main facial features are determined by the shape of the skull. Subtle details like the shape of the nose and ears, although influenced by age, sex, and ancestry, are artistic interpretations. Sculpted bust by StudioEIS based on forensic facial reconstruction by forensic artist Amanda Danning.

Sometimes...
BONES

SHOW UP *in* UNUSUAL PLACES

Douglas Owsley examines cranial bones
of a teen-aged English boy recovered from
a James Fort well that had been abandoned.
ca. 1608-1615. APVA Preservation Virginia/
Historic Jamestowne.

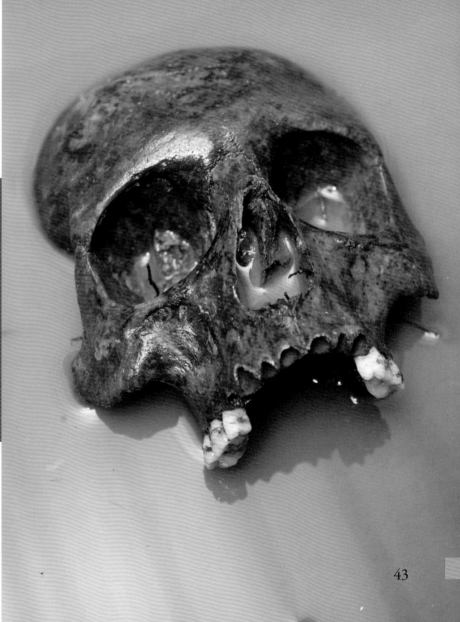

IMAGES, ESPECIALLY CONTROVERSIAL ONES, HAVE A DIRECT AND QUICK EMOTIONAL IMPACT THAT LINEAR TEXT ALONE LACKS. ON A FORMAL LEVEL, PHOTOGRAPHS TAKEN BY SCIENTIFIC PHOTOGRAPHERS ARE INDISTINGUISHABLE FROM ARTISTICALLY INTENDED IMAGES TAKEN BY A JOURNALIST. BUT UNLIKE PRIZE-WINNING PHOTOJOURNALISM, ARCHIVAL PHOTOS DEMAND A CAPTION

View of the three recovered cranial pieces and bones of the midface: frontal, basilar occipital, and left temporal, which were recovered from the well inside James Fort, Virginia.

FACE IN THE WELL/JAMESTOWN, VIRGINIA

The two and twentieth day of August, there died Captaine Bartholomew Gosnold. He was honorably buried, having all the Ordnance in the Fort shot off with many vollies of small shot. -GEORGE PERCY'S DIARY, 1607

46

Forensic anthropologist Douglas Owsley and postdoctoral fellow, Ashley McKeown, determine the age of this man and discuss stature differences by comparing his femur and tibia to contemporary bones. Bartholomew Gosnold was about 5'3" tall. The light colored femur and tibia are from the remains of a 5'9" male.

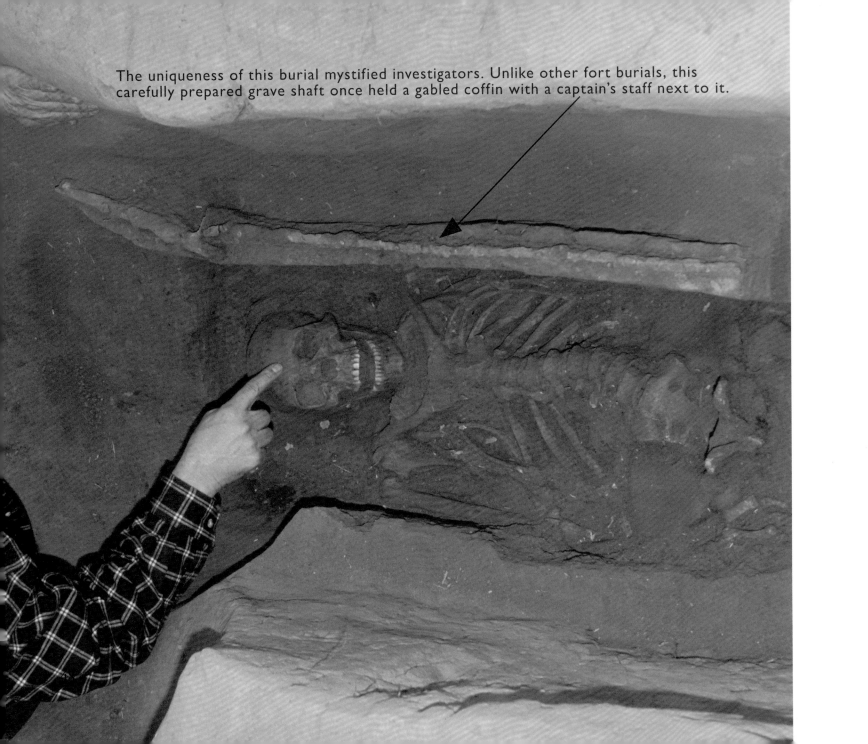

The uniqueness of this burial mystified investigators. Unlike other fort burials, this carefully prepared grave shaft once held a gabled coffin with a captain's staff next to it.

NO LONGER NAMELESS

No historic portraits of Bartholomew Gosnold exist.

Captain Bartholomew Gosnold,
life-size reconstruction by StudioEIS,
based on forensic facial reconstruction
by forensic artist Amanda Danning.

49

A PROBABLE ID

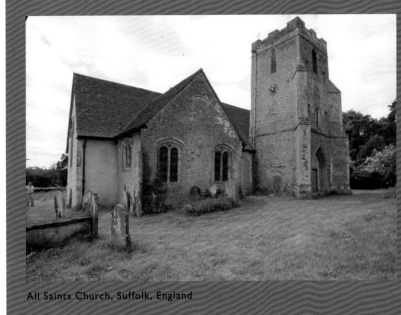

All Saints Church, Suffolk, England

Historical sources note that Gosnold died in his early thirties after a three-week illness. Such a quick illness would not have shown up in the skeleton.

If this is Gosnold's body, that would explain why no cause of death was apparent in the well-preserved remains. Even without a DNA match, investigators believe that the bones and burial data, supported by the colonists' writings, identify the man buried outside James Fort. All evidence—archaeological, forensic, and historical—points to Captain Bartholomew Gosnold.

Church records note that Gosnold's sister, Elizabeth Gosnold Tilney, was buried at All Saints Church under the floor of the chancel in an unmarked grave. In 2005, the Church of England granted permission for British and American scientists to excavate the probable site of her burial and sample the remains for DNA testing. The DNA did not match, but further analysis also revealed the bones were unlikely to have been his sister's remains.

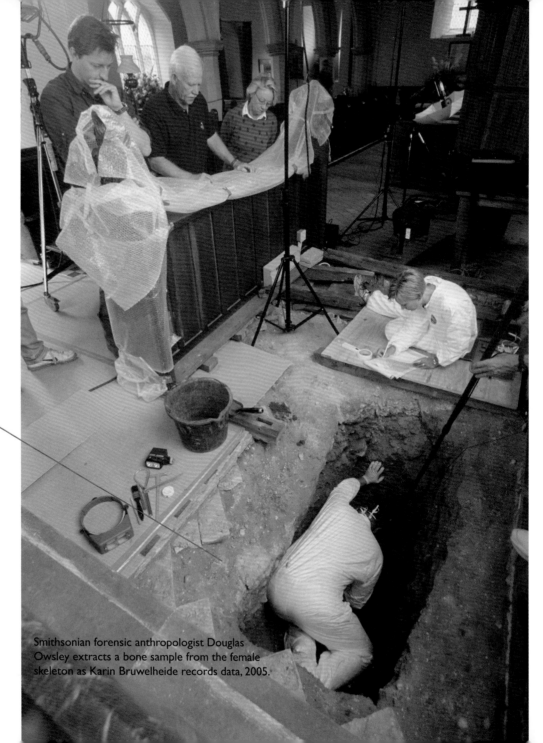

Smithsonian forensic anthropologist Douglas Owsley extracts a bone sample from the female skeleton as Karin Bruwelheide records data, 2005.

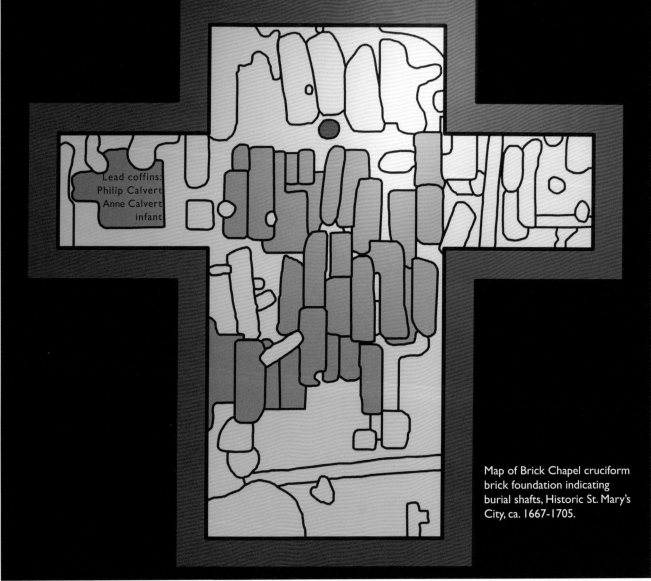

Lead coffins:
Philip Calvert
Anne Calvert
infant

Map of Brick Chapel cruciform
brick foundation indicating
burial shafts, Historic St. Mary's
City, ca. 1667-1705.

Team of forensic anthropologists and archaeologists excavate the remains and record data of a high status male found in a burial near the altar.

WE HAVE SEEN "UNUSUAL" BURIAL CONTEXTS WHERE PARTS OF SKELETONS HAVE BEEN RECOVERED FROM WELLS, TRASH PITS, CELLARS, AND TWO OR MORE TO A GRAVE.

Ruth Mitchell, archaeologist from Historic St Mary's City, excavating the remains.

THE BRICK CHAPEL CEMETERY SHOWS MORE TYPICAL BURIAL PRACTICES AND CHANGES IN BURIAL RITUAL AS ENGLISH SETTLEMENT IN THE CHESAPEAKE MATURED.

Feet and tibiae of female skeleton partially exposed underneath that of male skeleton unearthed from a later burial. The closeness of the female's feet and tibiae indicate the body was tightly shrouded.

Superior endplate of left humerus showing
expanded proximal metaphysis of infant with
abnormal mineralization of the bone due to
rickets. Lead Coffin Burial at Historic St. Mary's
City, Maryland, Brick Chapel, ca. 1683.

Karin Bruwelheide arranges the skeleton of a 5 to 6 month old infant buried in a small lead coffin.

WEALTH DID NOT SAVE
A VERY SICK INFANT

In 1992, archaeologists recovered the remains of an infant buried beneath the floor of the 17th-century Brick Chapel at St. Mary's City, Maryland. A small lead-sheathed coffin indicated that the baby belonged to a prominent family, but investigators had only the bones and burial clues to verify the identity as a Calvert infant.

The infant was suffering from a serious condition, rickets. Although a common plight of many children in the colonial Chesapeake, doctors of the time neither understood the malady nor knew how to treat it.

Vitamin and mineral deficiencies leave clear markers in bone. The skull, ribs, and long bones of this infant showed signs of the vitamin D deficiency, rickets. The identification of sex remains tentative, and DNA tests were inconclusive.

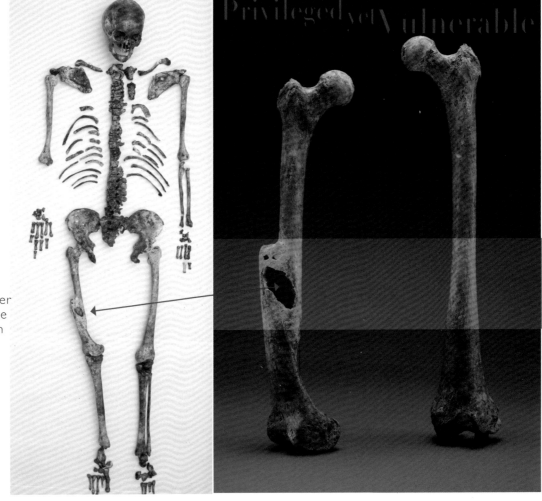

Privileged yet Vulnerable

Anne Wolseley Calvert was a socially prominent woman. She was the first wife of Philip Calvert, who came to America in 1657 to serve as chancellor and governor of Maryland. Misaligned, severe over-riding fracture of the right femur made her right leg shorter. A large draining sinus formed in the bone after the fracture and persisted until her death.

Reconstruction by StudioEIS based on facial reconstruction by forensic artist and anthropologist Sharon A. Long.

A large piece of a milk pan left on the chest clearly did not belong to the deceased but was used to DIG the shallow grave and FORCE HIS CORPSE into the pit

A ceramic milk pan showing rounded, polished, and fractured edges, was used for digging the grave.

The unevenly dug shallow pit was too short and narrow for the body, which was bent at the hips and knees. Whoever buried this boy packed the pit with clay and then filled the cellar with household trash. Lack of concern implies lack of connection to the household. The artifacts found in the trash layer just over the body date ca. 1663. Life-size reconstruction by StudioEIS based on forensic facial reconstruction by forensic artist Joanna Hughes.

The skeleton is REASSEMBLED

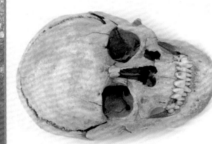

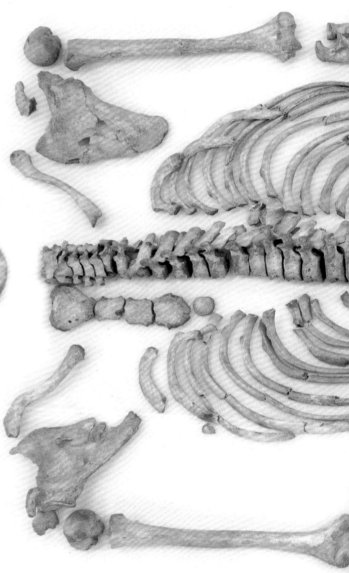

and photographed in its ENTIRETY.

LEAVY NECK BOY

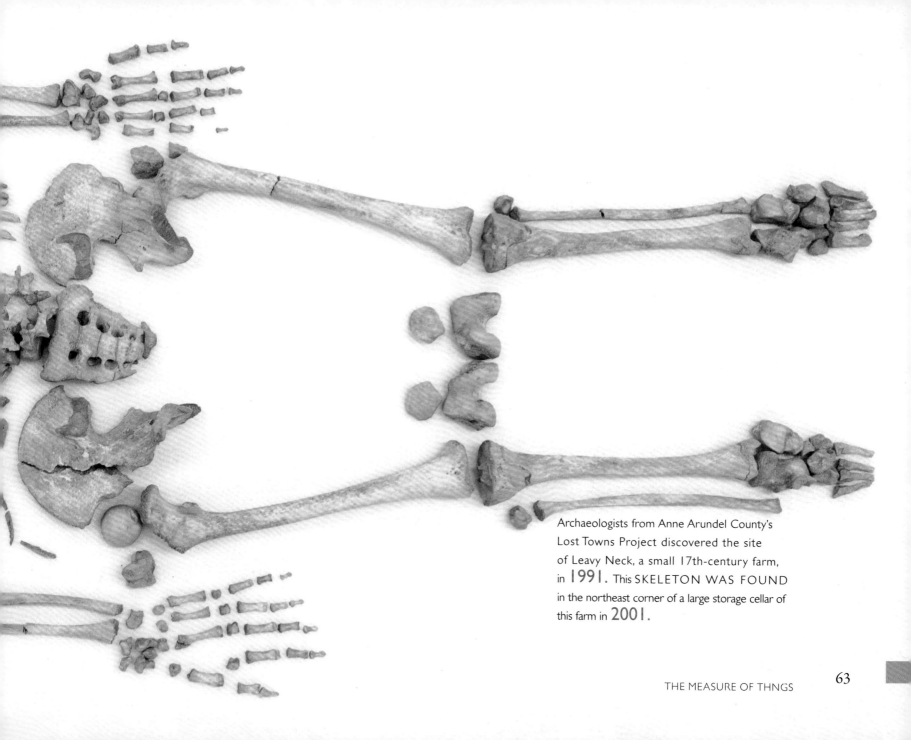

Archaeologists from Anne Arundel County's Lost Towns Project discovered the site of Leavy Neck, a small 17th-century farm, in 1991. This SKELETON WAS FOUND in the northeast corner of a large storage cellar of this farm in 2001.

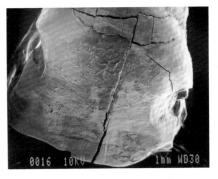

JORDAN'S JOURNEY PLANTATION
A magnified view of the "tailor's notches," grooves worn in both sides of a central maxillary incisor from holding needles and pins between her teeth. Female, Jordan's Point cemetery, Virginia, ca. 1625.

BONES
AND teeth
BEAR THE
BURDEN
OF PROOF

PATUXENT POINT
The skull of a young man with unusually well-defined pipe facets formed by clenching a pipe between his teeth. Calvert County, Maryland/Maryland Archaeological Conservation Laboratory/Jefferson Patterson Park & Museum, ca. 1660–1680.

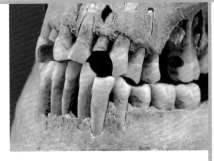

HISTORIC ST. MARY'S CITY
Skull of a woman who polished the enamel off her front teeth. Tooth whitening and cleaning recipes were acidic and abrasive. They included the use of salt and vinegar, as well as ingredients such as tobacco ashes, rubbed onto teeth with a cloth.
St. Mary's City, MD, ca. 1704–1730.

THE BONE
destruction
in the vertebrae is
SO SEVERE
that if this boy tried

to sit or stand upright,
his lower back would
BEND at a RIGHT ANGLE.

DARNALL'S CHANCE TOMB
Spinal column of a young male, age
12-14 years, with probable tuberculosis. Prince
George's County, Maryland, Darnall's Chance
House Museum, ca. 1700s.

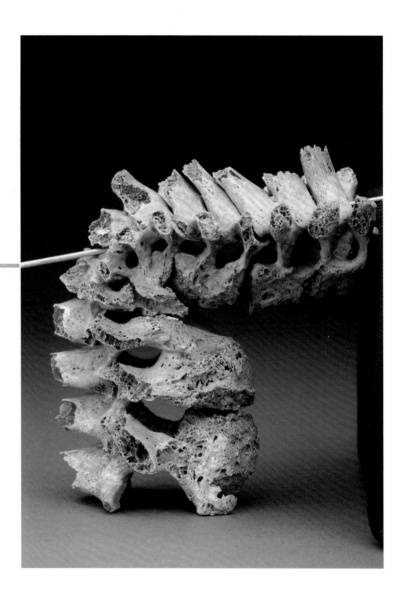

THE HUMAN CONDITION

It is said that every cemetery has two sections:

ONE FOR THE DEAD,
ONE FOR THE TRULY DEAD.

THE DEAD are those
whose graves people still visit,
THE TRULY DEAD are those
whose names have been forgotten.

Six young adult Caucasian males were buried
while their military unit was encamped in the
Centreville area during the Civil War, 1861-1865.
Karin Bruwelheide, Centreville, Virginia.

1861–1865

THE AMERICAN CIVIL WAR
COST 620,000 SOLDIERS THEIR LIVES

THERE WAS A STORY THAT CIVIL WAR SOLDIERS HAD BEEN BURIED NEAR THIS OLD CHURCH....

Plotting unmarked burials of Confederate soldiers, Emmanuel Lutheran Church, New Market, Virginia. The church vestry and the local chapter of the United Daughters of the Confederacy wanted to confirm the lore surrounding possible Civil War burials. Markers were ultimately placed on these graves.

CIVIL WAR

"I advise that all preparation be made for leaving Richmond tonight."

General Robert E. Lee to President Jefferson Davis

THE EXCAVATION

To begin, locate, map, and collect surface findings over the grave. First, establish a grid square. Attach a line level to the grid strings to determine vertical and horizontal location of items within the grave. Skim dirt from the surface within or directly around the burial until the human remains are encountered. Remove dirt one to two inches at a time...

Mapping the perimeters of grave shafts of unmarked and forgotten Civil War soldiers, Centreville, Virginia.

ABOUT ALL THAT A
PRIVATE SOLDIER EVER
KNOWS OF BATTLE......

EYES RIGHT, GUIDE
CENTER CLOSE UP,
GUIDE RIGHT, HALT,
FORWARD, RIGHT
OBLIQUE, LEFT
OBLIQUE, HALT,
FORWARD, GUIDE
CENTER, EYES RIGHT,
DRESS UP PROMPTLY
IN THE REAR, STEADY,
DOUBLE QUICK,
CHARGE BAYONETS,
FIRE AT WILL. — SAM WATKINS

MASON SURVIVED THE BATTLE OF SHILOH AS
A PRIVATE IN THE 11TH TENNESSEE CAVALRY REGIMENT.
THESE ARE THE BOOTS HE FOUGHT IN.

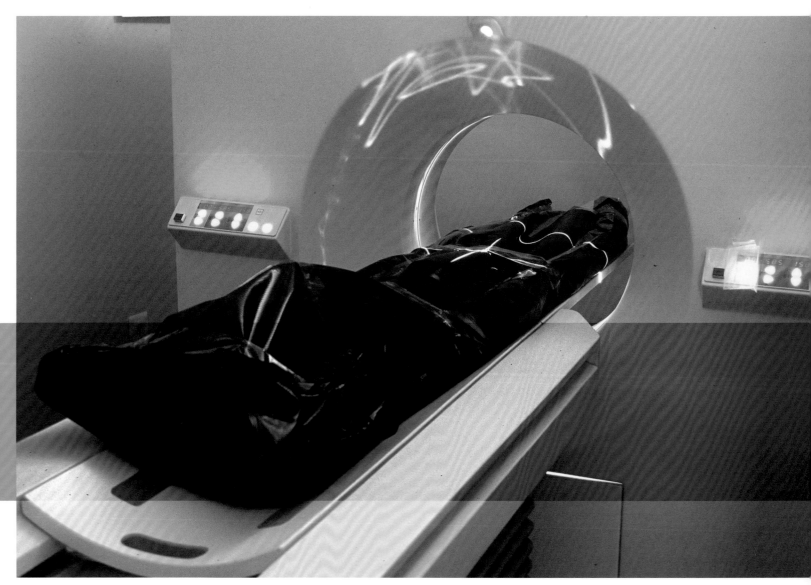

ISAAC NEWTON MASON/CIVIL WAR

To collect the data in bones, investigators start by visually inspecting the remains (gross examination), often with a magnifying lens. Scientific technologies, X-rays, CT scans, microscopic exams, and chemical analyses add information and provide an even closer look at the bones. CT Scan is a powerful nondestructive evaluation technique for producing 2D and 3D cross-sectional images of an object from flat X-ray images. Characteristics of the internal structure of an object such as dimensions, shape, internal defects, and density are readily available from CT images.

Remains of Isaac Newton Mason

Fairview Cemetery, Culpeper, Virginia

"NOBLER CHAMPION HAS FALLEN."
-GEN. J.E.B. STUART

On October 21, 2001, after 138 years, the wish of Confederate Captain William Downs Farley was finally granted.

His remains had been buried in the Culpeper, Virginia cemetery and were finally going home to Laurens, South Carolina.

Curiosity and desire to solve a case consumes you so much that it not only occupies your days but many of your nights. -DOUGLAS OWSLEY

Captain Farley Headstone

feet

Footstone

Location of artifacts, relative to the approximate position of the skeletal soil shadow

● MILK GLASS BUTTON

● VERTICAL NAIL

\ HORIZONTAL NAIL

feet

CAPTAIN FARLEY

was mortally wounded while sitting astride his horse discussing orders with Col. Matthew Calbraith Butler. A cannon ball passed through his horse and severed his right leg at the knee. When being carried off the field, Farley asked Lt. John Rhett to bring him his severed leg. Rhett later described the incident in his journal.

'It is an old friend, gentlemen, and I do not wish to part from it.' -WILL FARLEY

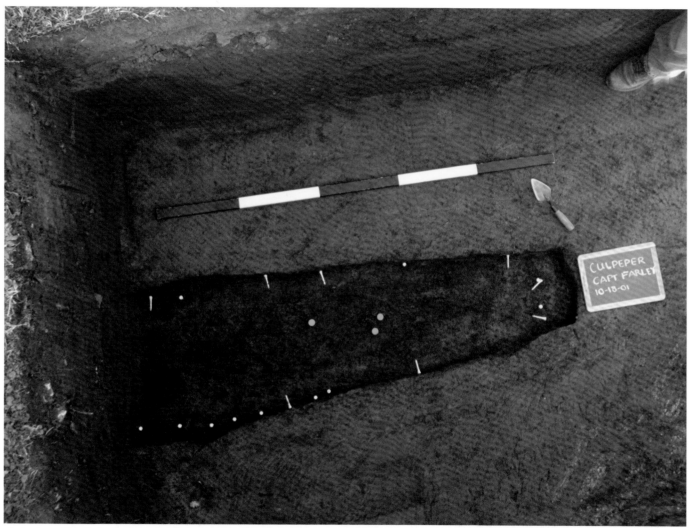

A shadow of black dirt in the red clay showed the captain lying with his left leg intact, but his right leg severed at the knee. The imprint of his severed limb was clearly visible, resting close beside the left leg.

Collecting osteological data is not a one-person endeavor. The success of our detailed work and methodology depends on experienced researchers and students in training. No team is ever complete without the expertise of the science photographer. We record a couple thousand computerized observations and measurements for each complete skeleton as well as taking hundreds of digital photographs. A team of ours can **handle forty skeletons in a week.** —DOUGLAS OWSL

Timberlake cast iron coffin: Karin Bruwelheide and student intern Brittney Tatchell analyze the remains of A.B. Timberlake in the Anthropology Lab, National Museum of Natural History, Smithsonian Institution.

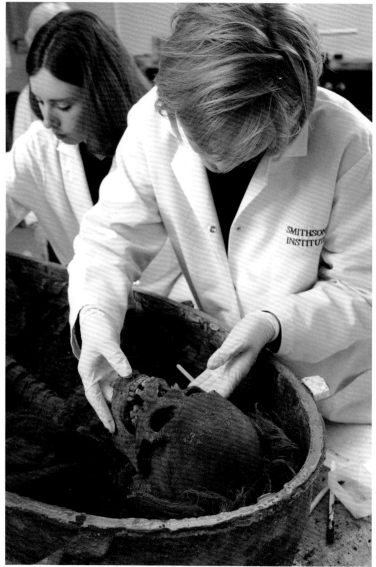

81

Wrought iron shackles, found in an abandoned well, with one anklet chiseled apart, 2nd quarter 18th century, Pettus site, James City County, Virginia.

82

UNNAMED BUT NOT UNKNOWN

The lack of historic documentation makes the identification of bones all the more important for people of African ancestry. Skeletons give equal voice to people of the past. Human remains offer compelling proof that men and women of African ancestry lived and died during the earliest years of colonial settlement in the Chesapeake.

Dental remains offer important personal evidence about the major African tribal groups central to the cultural formation of the United States. Dental modifications verify specific links between African populations and their American-born descendants. Advertisements for runaway slaves referred to persons with filed teeth as African-born, supporting claims that these remains represent first generation Africans in the New World.

Labial view of intentionally modified left lateral maxillary incisor, African, 17th century, St. Mary's City, Maryland.

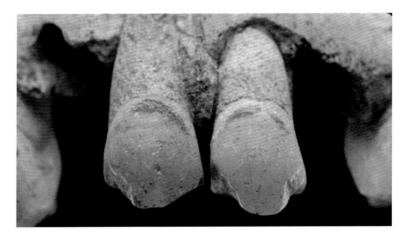

Adult male with filed central maxillary incisors that match a pattern identified as West African. Grenada, West Indies, ca. 1700s–1830s.

Side-by-side view of femur and tibia joint surfaces. Male with dislocation of right knee that resulted in severe erosion and macroporosity of the joint surfaces. Rutland African Slave Cemetery, Virginia, 1800s.

Right lateral view of vertebral column, male with Diffuse Idiopathic Skeletal Hyperostosis, DISH, a form of degenerative arthritis characterized by unique flowing calcification along the sides of the vertebrae of the spine. Harleigh Knoll site, Maryland, 1700s.

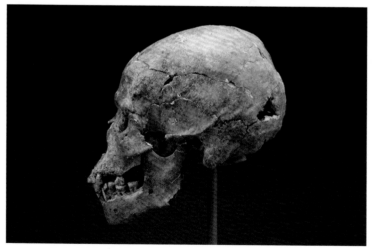

Left lateral view of skull, male, African ancestry, Pettus site, Virginia

Harleigh Knoll is a site in an estuary area of Talbot County on Maryland's Eastern Shore. The distinguishing feature of this natural sandy mound is a forgotten colonial cemetery containing individuals of African and European descent buried side by side.

THE NEXT GENERATION OF BONE BIOGRAPHERS

Students and teachers from three Eastern Shore high schools in Talbot and Queen Anne's counties, assisted Douglas Owsley, Dana Kollmann, and other professionals with excavation work. This included cleaning, photographing, and measuring each set of remains before the bones were transported to the lab.

PHOTOGRAPHIC **IMAGE RECORD**

Multiple photographic views of the skull are taken in frontal, left and right laterals, posterior, superior, and inferior views in

THE STANDARD FRANKFORT HORIZONTAL (FH)

anatomical position.

The **FRANKFORT HORIZONTAL**, eye to ear plane, is a CONSISTENT AND REPRODUCIBLE POSITION.

CRANIAL LANDMARKS

In order to describe the orientation of skeletal and dental structures and their component parts in 3D, uniformity of description is necessary.

Anterior view of skull
Black female, 15.5-16.5 years
Harleigh Knoll site, Maryland.

Anterior view of skull
Black female, 30-36 years
Harleigh Knoll site, Maryland.

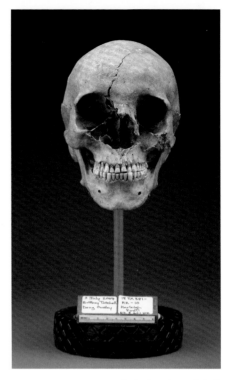

Anterior view of skull
Black female, 60+ years
Harleigh Knoll site, Maryland.

I am a BLACK woman

Burial #1 Harleigh Knoll site, Maryland.

tall as a cypress
strong
beyond all definition still
defying place
and time   -MARI EVANS

In November 2004, the remains of a young African woman were found in a crumbling hexagonal wooden coffin at a former tobacco plantation on Maryland's Eastern Shore. Her cause of death remains a mystery, but her skeleton tells of a hard life of physical labor.

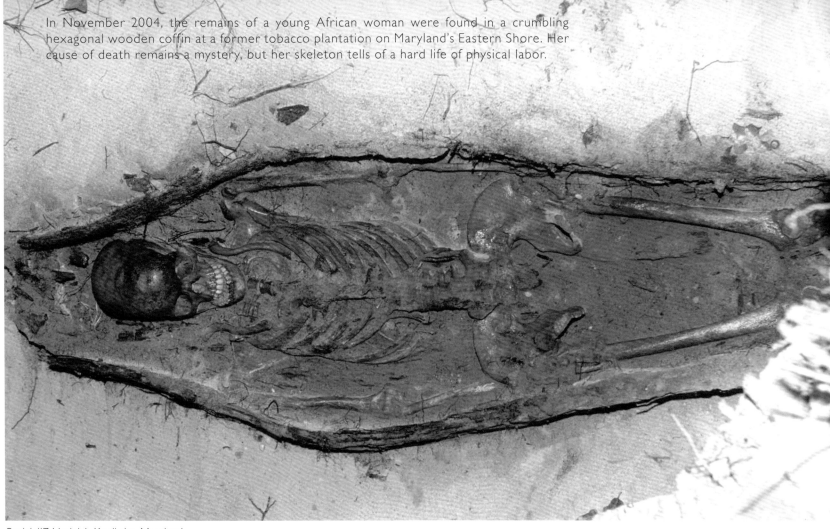

Burial #7 Harleigh Knoll site, Maryland.

It is possible to rebuild in clay what a person's face might have looked like in life... she now returns our gaze.

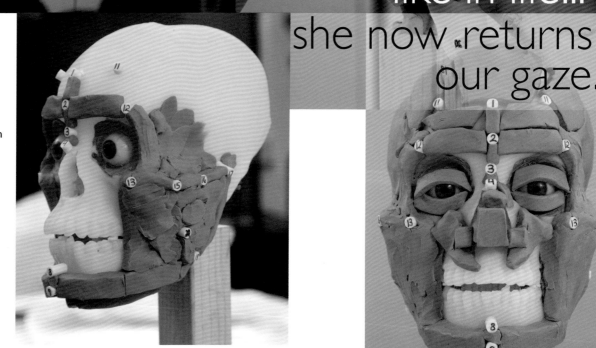

Small pegs scaled to tissue depths are glued to a replica of the skull on preset facial landmarks. Strips of clay made to match the height of the pegs fill the gaps between each peg. Artificial eyes are placed in the sockets, lips shaped, and facial contours smoothed.

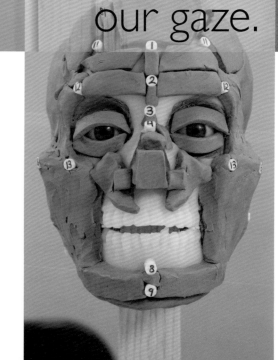

AFRICAN LIVES/HARLEIGH KNOLL SITE

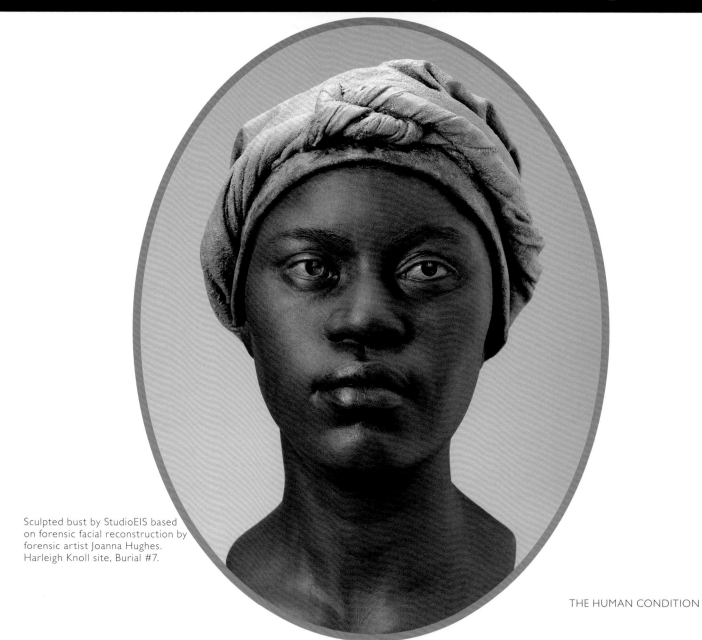

Sculpted bust by StudioEIS based
on forensic facial reconstruction by
forensic artist Joanna Hughes.
Harleigh Knoll site, Burial #7.

FORENSIC CASEWORK

" The image is purposely absent of any type, leaving the illustration alone to serve as the clue-giver. "
-GREG PALAZZOLO

They had been working from morning to night at the morgue in Zagreb, when Mario says to Owsley,

"There's something I need to show you."

In crime scene investigator Dana Kollmann's photo, the evil reality of the Bleiburg Massacre is highlighted by shafts of golden sunlight breaking through a window near the rafters in a dingy attic room above a morgue. Waves and waves of glistening black garbage bags stuffed with skulls and other bones, the only shroud these countless dead had ever known. The sight of Owsley in a white lab coat holding the open end of death in one hand and reaching into the void with the other is hard to reconcile.

Douglas Owsley examines WWII victims found in an attic at the University of Zagreb Medical School, Croatia

AN ATTIC ROOM IN ZAGREB

The Bleiburg Massacre took place in May 1945, near the end of World War II. Tens of thousands fleeing the defeated independent State of Croatia, were planning to surrender to the Allies, but were forcibly turned away only to meet the wrath of the communist Yugoslav army.

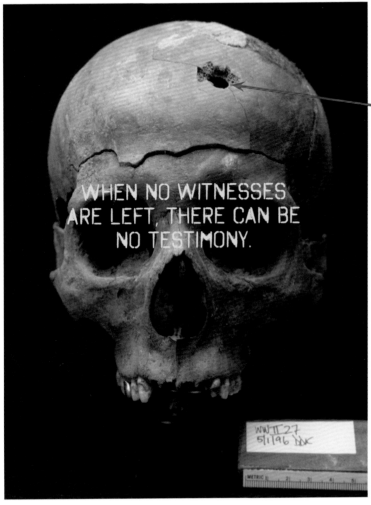

WHEN NO WITNESSES ARE LEFT, THERE CAN BE NO TESTIMONY.

-HANNAH ARENDT

Skull showing execution style gunshot exit wound, University of Zagreb Medical School, Croatia

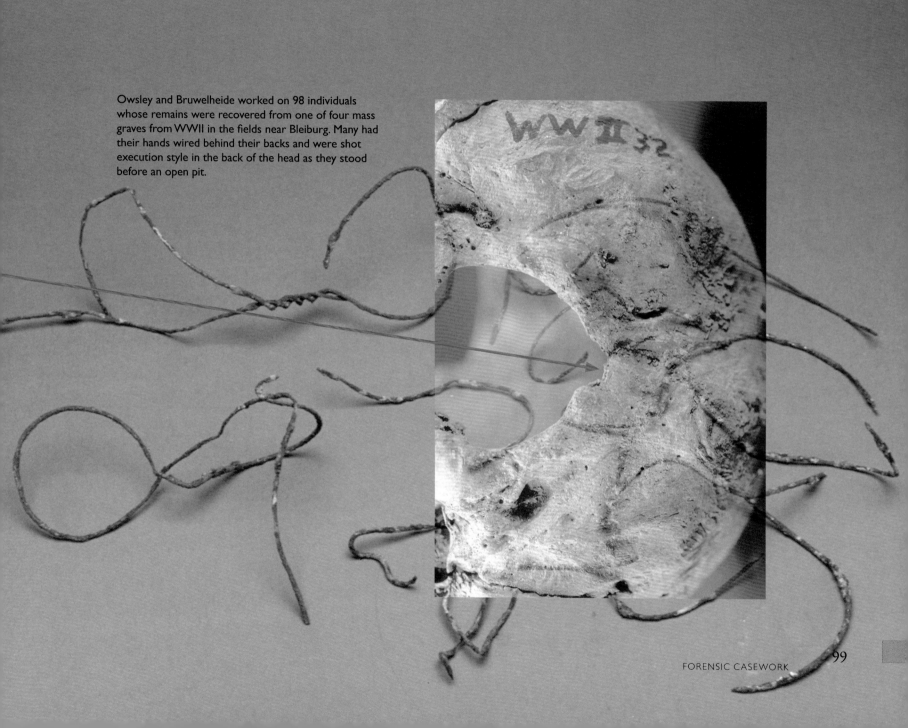

Owsley and Bruwelheide worked on 98 individuals whose remains were recovered from one of four mass graves from WWII in the fields near Bleiburg. Many had their hands wired behind their backs and were shot execution style in the back of the head as they stood before an open pit.

WW II 32

The following goals of forensic anthropological
investigations of war crimes are considered as acts
of justice and reparation: recuperation of human
remains by exhumation; identification
of mass graves; identification of victims
when possible; determination of the cause of death;
provision of material evidence and expert witness
opinions.

Traveling to the morgue in Zagreb.

Croatia

THE ROAD TO GLINA

"An hour after leaving Zagreb and traveling south toward the current border between Croatia and Bosnia, we were overwhelmed by the devastation caused by the conflict that began in August 1991. The Croatian military had regained this territory from Serbian forces in August 1995. Small villages consist almost entirely of ruins of former homes; partially destroyed walls of concrete and terra cotta blocks are the remnants of sturdy houses that are generations old. Roofless and without doors or windows, the houses bear the scars of war created by rockets and artillery. Also visible are the pockmarks from grenade fragments and automatic weapons. Fires consumed all the combustible parts of the homes, including the furniture and other comforts and keepsakes. In the early spring of 1996, the fields of these farming communities remain untilled because they are still seeded with land mines. Although a few residents are beginning to return and rebuild, most are still absent, having fled to places of safety. Other villagers are absent because they lost their lives during acts of brutality when they would not desert their homes."

Recovery and Identification of Civilian Victims of War in Croatia by Douglas Owsley, et al.

Propaganda on wall of abandoned home, Glina, Croatia.

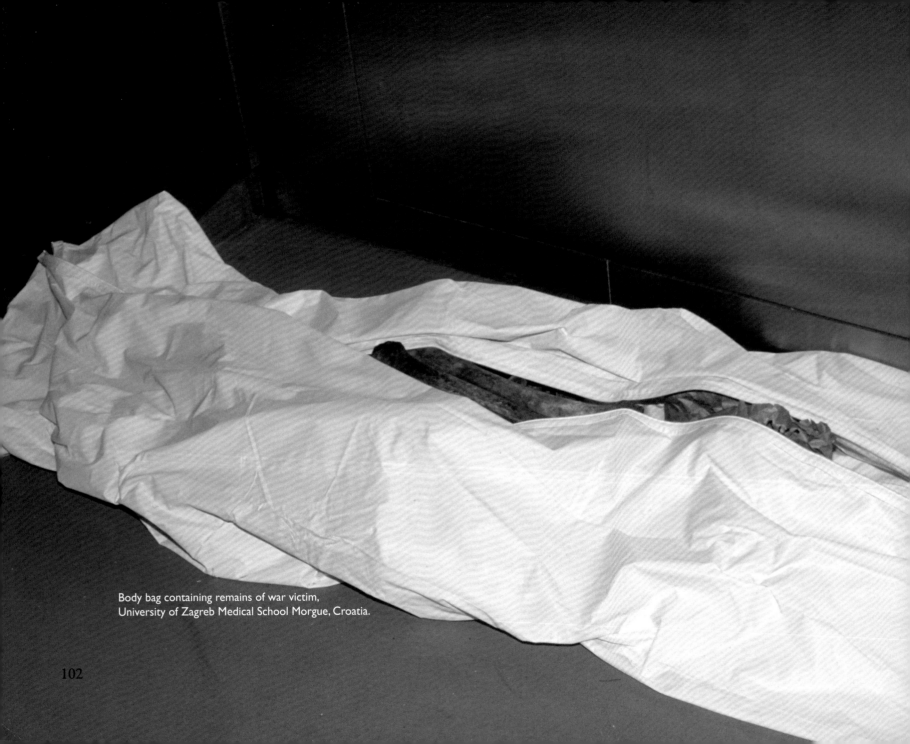

Body bag containing remains of war victim,
University of Zagreb Medical School Morgue, Croatia.

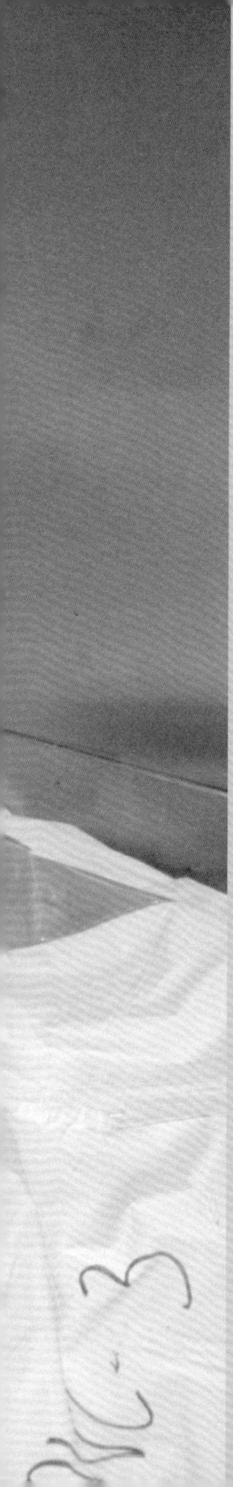

Spaljeno selo
Pas lutalica njuši
pougljene kosti

-Vladimir Devidé

In the burned-out village
a wounded stray dog
sniffing charred bones

TAKING STOCK Mapping and surveying the
BODY COUNT Determining the age,
SCIENTIFIC RECORD Entering all informa
RAPHIC EVIDENC

Partially healed sharp force injury to the cranial vault. Not the cause of death.

FORENSIC ANTHROPOLOGY/CROATIA

Douglas Owsley and Dr. Lee Jantz work meticulously to establish the unique data necessary for positive identification. In background, Dr. Richard Jantz using a digitizer to measure skulls.

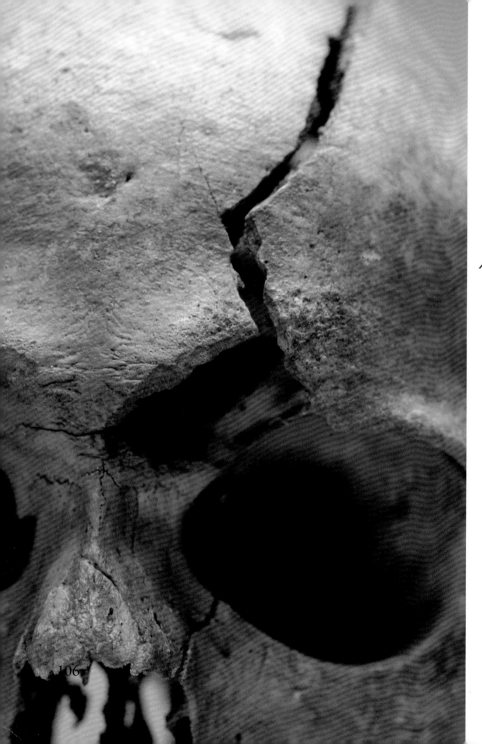

106

SMALL AND
FRAGILE ITEMS,
SUCH AS TEETH,
BULLETS,
PERSONAL EFFECTS

*a small piece of paper
found on a victim*

ARE OFTEN CRITICAL IN
THE IDENTIFICATION OF THE DECEASED
AND THE DETERMINATION OF THE
CAUSE AND MANNER OF DEATH.

Exit gunshot wound, Catholic Cemetery, where bodies
were hidden. Glina, Croatia.

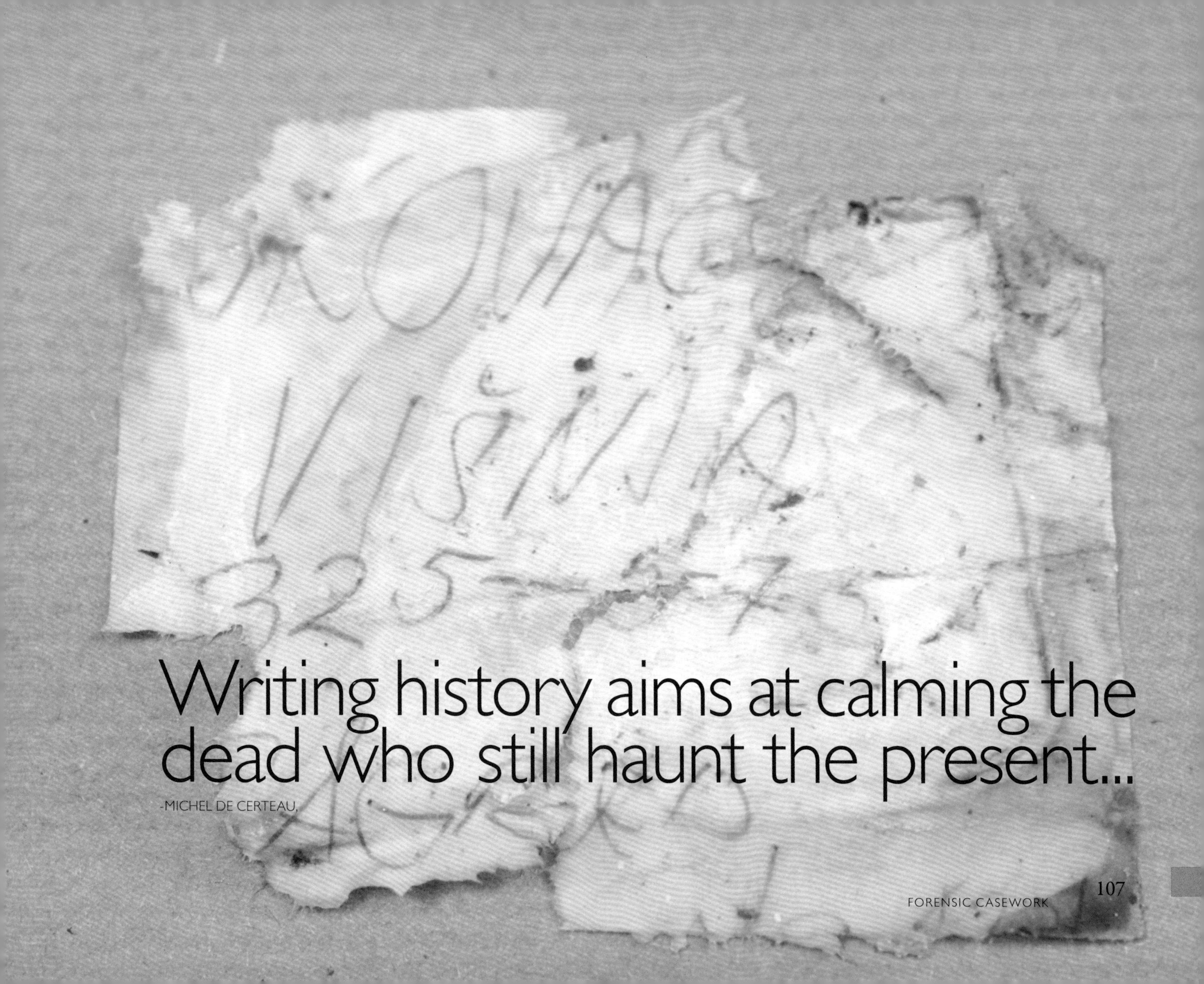

Writing history aims at calming the dead who still haunt the present...

-MICHEL DE CERTEAU,

107

Portable studio equipment had been brought from the Smithsonian Institution to photograph bones and other burial artifacts.

Identification criteria depended heavily on descriptive information provided by friends and relatives. Showing family members photographs of clothing and personal items was essential to completing these unpleasant but necessary tasks.

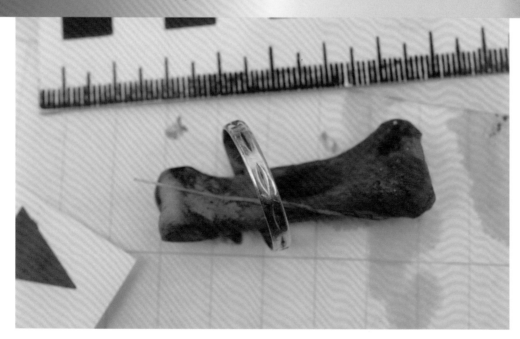

Proximal phalanx with ring, *in situ*, Glina, Croatia.

High velocity bullets found in remains.

ON THE FLOOR WERE
NUMEROUS 7.62 MM
SHELL CASINGS THAT
CAN BE FIRED FROM
AN SKS OR AK-47
AUTOMATIC WEAPON.

Bullets of high velocity weapons
shatter the skull in a pattern distinct
from low velocity weapons.

The mass disaster involved three of the Smithsonian's forensic anthropologists and science photographer Chip Clark. After a cadaver dog could not find the last four unaccounted bodies, Owsley used a piece of rebar to probe the mud, locating the remains, which were stacked one on top of the other in a single grave. The remains were those of Branch Davidians who died during the raid on the compound and had been buried by fellow Davidians in the under-ground firearms range.

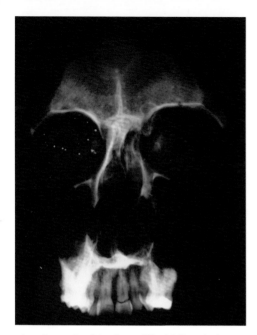

A radiograph of the face of David Koresh shows a gunshot entrance wound to the forehead.

The skull exhibits extensive fracturing as well as burning. The occipital bone in the back of the skull shows the bullet's exit, characterized by external beveling of the margin and loss of outer table with exposure of the underlying cancellous bone. The pattern of burning and fracturing indicates that the gunshot wound occurred at close range before the fire that swept through the compound had reached the body. The gunshot wound was not caused by law enforcement.

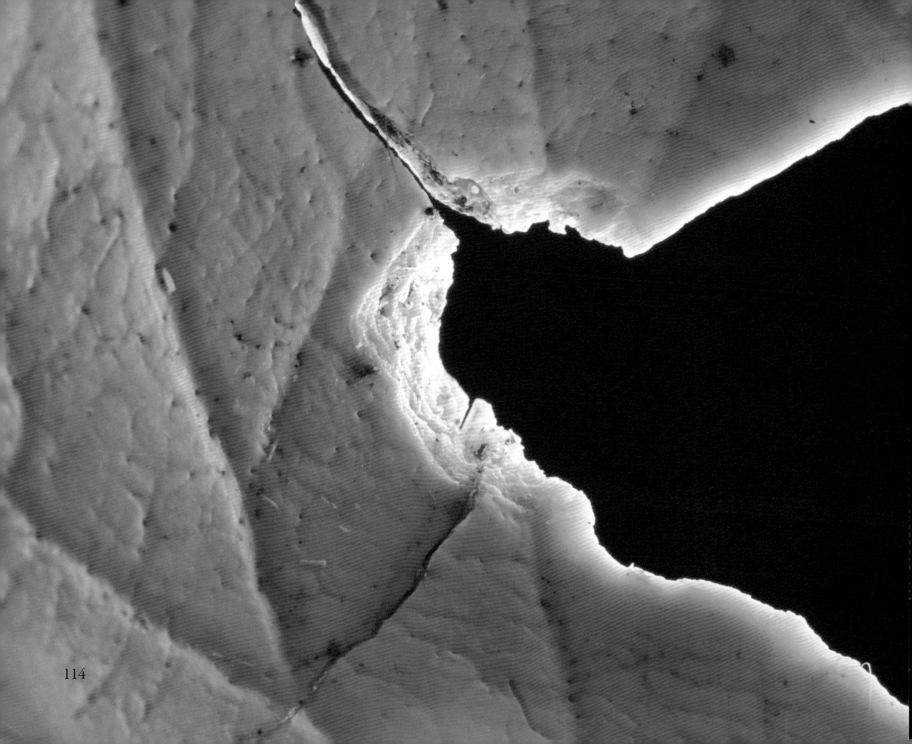

114

ON 6 APRIL 2004, INCOMPLETE SKELETAL REMAINS OF A HOMICIDE VICTIM WERE TRANSPORTED TO THE MUSEUM OF NATURAL HISTORY FOR FORENSIC ANTHROPOLOGICAL ANALYSIS.

THE REMAINS HAD BEEN IDENTIFIED BY DENTAL RECORDS. THE PURPOSE OF THIS EXAMINATION WAS TO PROVIDE INFORMATION REGARDING PERIMORTEM FRACTURING AND POSTMORTEM BREAKAGE.

ASSESSMENT OF THE NATURE OF GUNSHOT WOUNDS HELPS RECONSTRUCT EVENTS SURROUNDING THE DEATH. THERE ARE VARIOUS COMPONENTS OF THE ANALYSIS OF GUNSHOT WOUNDS BASED ON EXTENSIVE OBSERVATIONS OF KNOWN CASES: ENTRANCE AND EXIT FRACTURE PATTERNS, ANGLE AND PATH, RANGE OF FIRE AND VELOCITY, AND CALIBER OF THE BULLET.

Steve Jabo, Preparator Specialist, Smithsonian Institution, makes silicone molds and prepares cut edges on the cranium for tool marks analysis.

2 GUNSHOT WOUNDS
AND A DECAPITATION

ONE BULLET
entered through the right eye orbit and exited through the left side of the lower face.

A SECOND BULLET
entered the left side of the superior vault and exited through the inferior-posterior aspect of the right side of the head.

Cuts in the cranium indicated that a
SHARP BLADED TOOL
was involved in the crime.

TOOL MARK ANALYSIS IDENITFYING A SPECIFIC IMPLEMENT

Chop marks to the posterior occipital and first cervical vertebra indicate that the body was decapitated using a bladed tool such as a hatchet, axe, or machete. This high resolution image confirms a perfect match between the grooves in the bone and the imperfections of this axe blade.

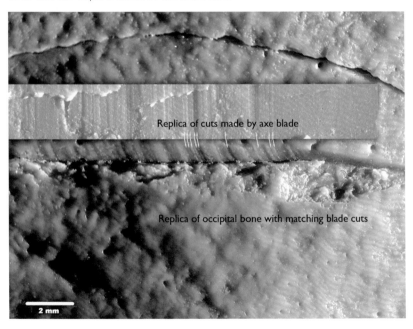

Replica of cuts made by axe blade

Replica of occipital bone with matching blade cuts

2 mm

Two bladed chops cut completely through the middle of the occipital squamous. A third chop cut through the outer table of the occipital, and a fourth grazed and marked the outer table of the inferior occipital squamous.

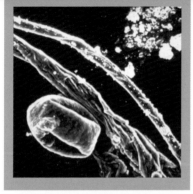

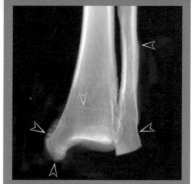

left to right:
CT scan of fiber
Scanning electron microscopy
X-ray imaging of tibia and fibula

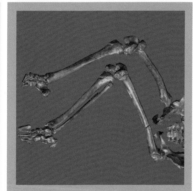
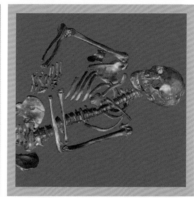

left to right:
Structured light
scanning and resulting
3D image.

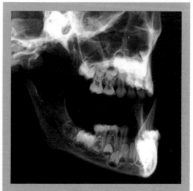

left to right:
Sliding caliper measuring neonate femur
CT scanning
Standard radiograph, dentition

APPLIED SCIENCE

A mutual dependency and caring come into view through the gifted lens of the photographer; the hands of the present, ever visible, in service and with reverence; the human remains stark, inescapable.

Martha Kate Spradley, doctoral student, uses a 3D digitizer to measure a cranium. Cádiz, Spain, 2005.

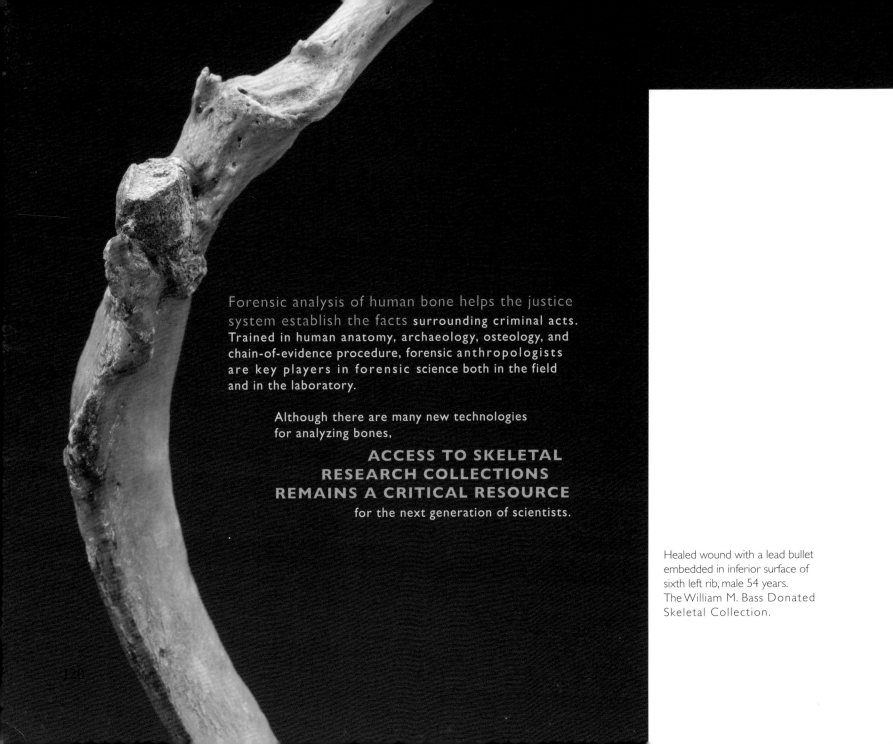

Forensic analysis of human bone helps the justice
system establish the facts surrounding criminal acts.
Trained in human anatomy, archaeology, osteology, and
chain-of-evidence procedure, forensic anthropologists
are key players in forensic science both in the field
and in the laboratory.

Although there are many new technologies
for analyzing bones,

ACCESS TO SKELETAL
RESEARCH COLLECTIONS
REMAINS A CRITICAL RESOURCE

for the next generation of scientists.

Healed wound with a lead bullet
embedded in inferior surface of
sixth left rib, male 54 years.
The William M. Bass Donated
Skeletal Collection.

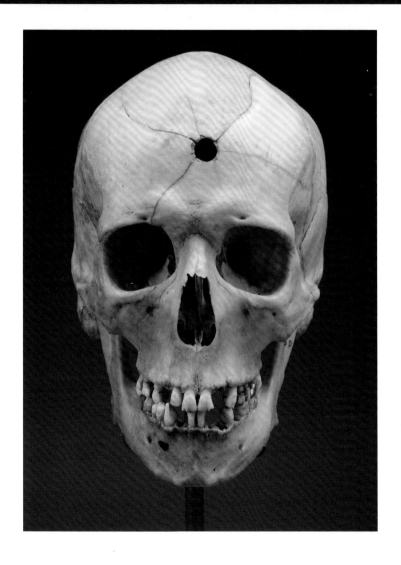

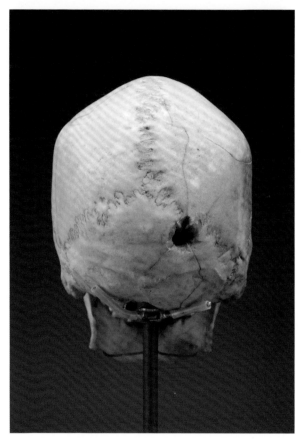

Anterior and posterior views of a skull with a sharply defined entrance gunshot wound in the frontal bone with radiating fractures, and an externally bevelled exit wound in the occipital bone, male 73 years. The William M. Bass Donated Skeletal Collection.

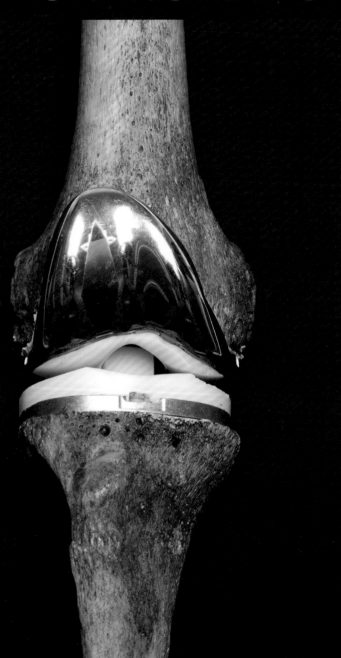

Knee replacement, male 63 years. The
William M. Bass Donated Skeletal
Collection.

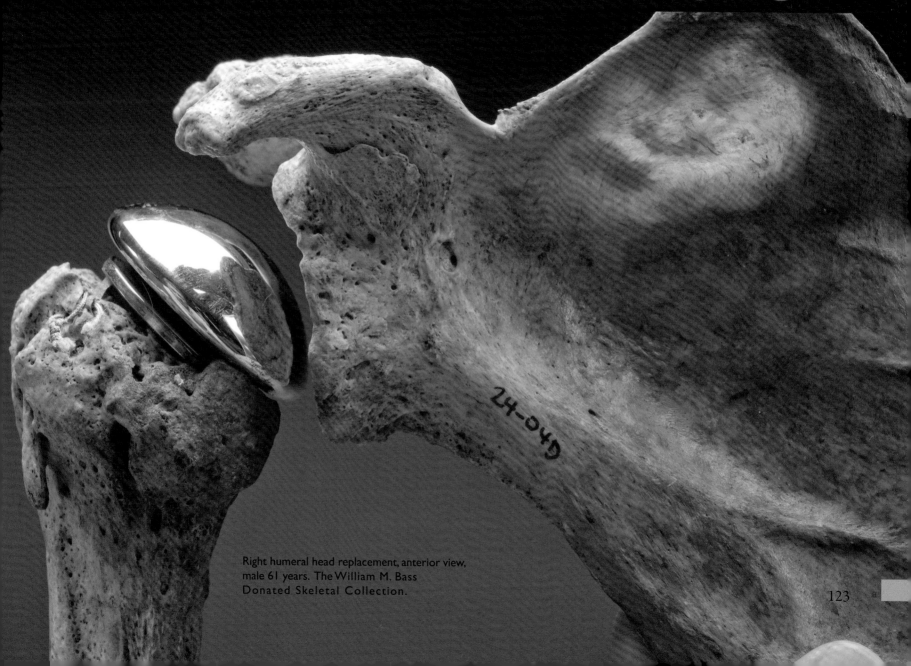

Right humeral head replacement, anterior view,
male 61 years. The William M. Bass
Donated Skeletal Collection.

PATHOLOGY

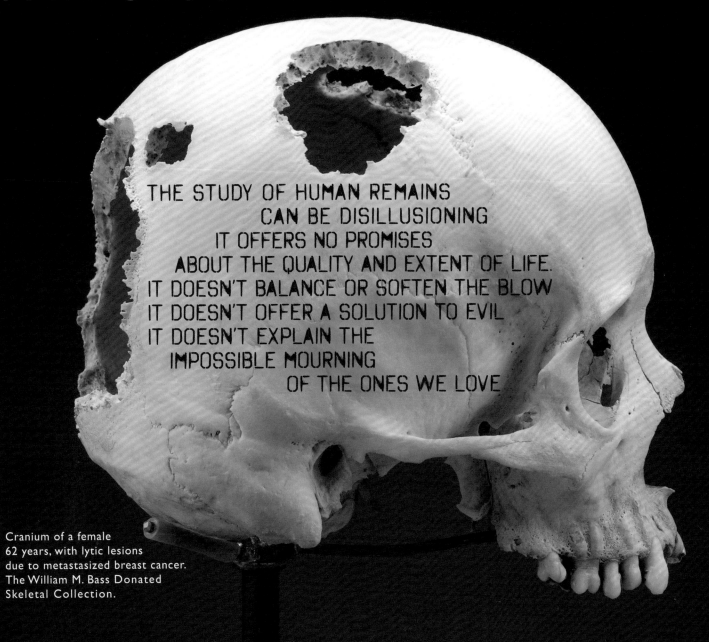

THE STUDY OF HUMAN REMAINS
CAN BE DISILLUSIONING
IT OFFERS NO PROMISES
ABOUT THE QUALITY AND EXTENT OF LIFE.
IT DOESN'T BALANCE OR SOFTEN THE BLOW
IT DOESN'T OFFER A SOLUTION TO EVIL
IT DOESN'T EXPLAIN THE
IMPOSSIBLE MOURNING
OF THE ONES WE LOVE

Cranium of a female
62 years, with lytic lesions
due to metastasized breast cancer.
The William M. Bass Donated
Skeletal Collection.

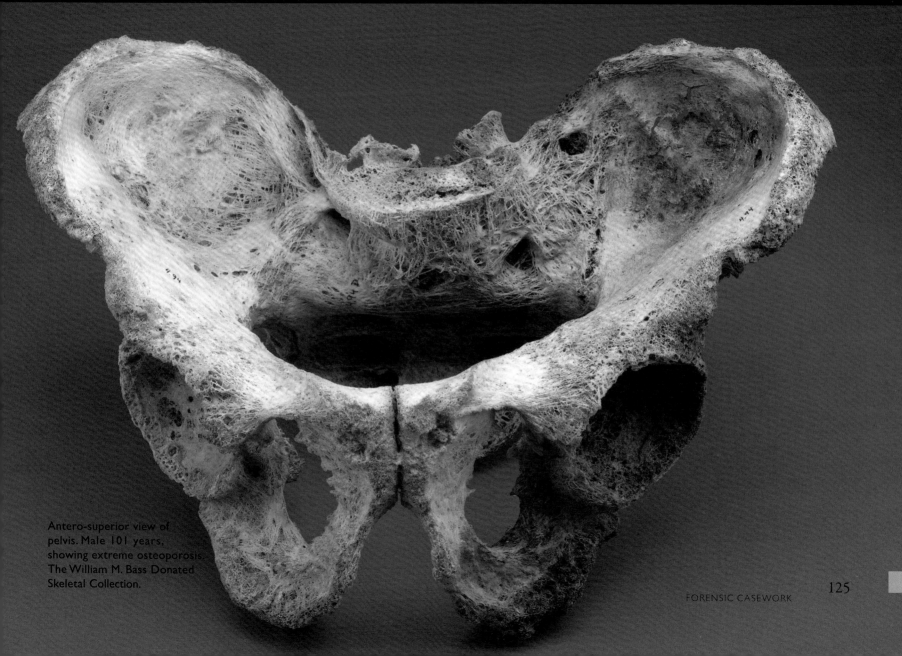

Antero-superior view of pelvis. Male 101 years, showing extreme osteoporosis. The William M. Bass Donated Skeletal Collection.

Thinking of the dark haul of all
            the wide-eyed once familiar faces
now sinking or sunken
            Thinking of all the souls now settling
            like ballast
                        into the Chesapeake
into the empire of the whistling swan

From "Hymn to the Chesapeake" by Robert P. Arthur

126

Whatever means individuals may have to shield themselves from the knowledge of facts, societies cannot long exist in opposition to truth known in the heart. What we leave behind and in front of us matters. Truth, fairness, restitution, reconciliation, and forgiveness—these are everywhere the pillars of justice.

The narrative told by bones to the keen observer draws human ends—and means—into the light of truth.

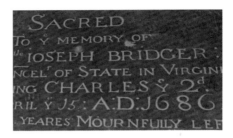

JOSEPH BRIDGER

Colonel Joseph Bridger was one of the ten wealthiest Virginians of his time. Between 1657 and his death in 1686, he held many prominent public offices and military commissions. He served as a councilor to the King of England until his death, at the age of 58. Joseph Bridger was first buried in 1686 at his White Marsh Plantation not far from the James River. His body was moved in 1894 to Historic St. Luke's Church in Smithfield, Virginia, the oldest standing English church in America.

In early 2007, at the request of 62 descendants, "Grandfather" Bridger's remains were temporarily exhumed from Saint Luke's Church and taken to the Smithsonian laboratory. Osteological analysis showed that Joseph Bridger suffered afflictions that would have made daily life miserable. In addition to dental disease and gout, his bones were laced with lead, a condition common among those who used pewter plates and utensils during colonial times. Lead intake increased with wealth, so a very high lead content in 17th-century bone indicates a person of means. When his remains were tested in 2007, his bone lead levels were 149 ppm—more than seven times the average level today.

CLAUDIUS CROZET 1790-1864

Crozet was a French engineer who emigrated to America to assist the new government in building the Blue Ridge Railroad and its tunnels in Virginia. He also helped found the Virginia Military Institute (VMI). When the monument over Crozet's burial was being moved to another location on the VMI campus, the officials in charge requested that his remains be examined. The Crozet cast iron coffin is one of several of its kind brought to the Smithsonian's National Museum of Natural History(NMNH) anthropology laboratory. The opening of the Crozet coffin and review of its contents was filmed by the History Channel's videography team. Research on cast iron coffins is a multidisciplinary team effort involving forensic anthropologists, forensic pathologists, historical archaeologists, historiographers, costume historians and genealogists.

The CAST IRON COFFIN was one of the best "body preserving" burial containers manufactured in North America in the 19th century. Protruding flanges encircle the top and bottom sections which are joined with a lead seal and then bolted together. The correct recovery and careful examination of cast iron coffins and their contents offers an exceptional opportunity to obtain information on social customs, dress, and health, including nutrition, disease, trauma, and activity patterns.

WILLIAM TAYLOR WHITE

In 2005, construction workers in Washington, DC, unexpectedly unearthed an iron coffin containing the remains of a boy. Because the iron coffin was air-tight, his remains were virtually mummified. The development of the boy's teeth indicated he had died in his mid-teens. His clothing was dated to the 1850s. Museum researchers narrowed their search of census records and obituaries to a single name and then constructed a 788-person family tree, a diagram that covered an entire wall. William Taylor White was an orphan from Accomack County, Virginia, who had moved to Washington to attend Columbian College (now George Washington University). He died on January 24, 1852, at age 15, most likely from an infection exacerbated by a heart condition. Researchers were able to confirm William's identity by comparing his DNA with that of a living relative, Linda Dwyer of Lancaster, Pennsylvania. Elated Smithsonian researchers called Linda with the news, "It's you! It's you!" Dwyer said she was flabbergasted to discover "a whole bunch of cousins" she didn't even know she had. The computerized drawing of William's face looked so much like Linda that she could have been his sister.

CÁDIZ FORENSIC PROJECT
RAMÓN POWER Y GIRALT
A commission of scholars and scientists was formed by the Puerto Rican government to identify the remains of Ramón Power y Giralt, the country's first diplomat and member of the 1812 Spanish Court. In 1813, shortly after signing the Spanish Constitution claiming independence from Napoleon, Power died of yellow fever and was buried in Spain. His remains were eventually entombed in a small crypt within the Oratorio de San Felipe Neri church in Cádiz, Spain, along with the remains of ten other diplomats. Nearly 200 years later, the commission sought to identify Power's body and return it to his country of origin. The investigation employed multiple lines of evidence in the identification of his skeleton, including comparison of osteological profiles with available historical information, stable carbon isotope analysis, and mtDNA comparisons with bone samples taken from the Power family vault in Puerto Rico. Two potential candidates were identified and eventually one was selected based on its genetic code. The crypt was opened on March 19, 2002.

VICE ADMIRAL BARTHOLOMEW
GOSNOLD 1572–1607
Bartholomew Gosnold was an enthusiastic promoter of colonization. An English lawyer and explorer, he first led an expedition to New England in 1602. He named Cape Cod after the abundant fish he found there and Martha's Vineyard for his daughter. Gosnold captained the Godspeed, one of three ships that sailed for North America in 1606. He landed in what became known as Virginia and settled James Fort, later known as Jamestown, the first British colony in North America. Douglas Owsley, Karin Bruwelheide and photographer Chip Clark traveled to England on June 13, 2005, to obtain DNA samples that would help confirm the identity of Gosnold's remains. A DNA sample was collected from what was hoped to be the remains of one of Gosnold's maternal relatives. Elizabeth Tilney, Gosnold's sister (70 years at death), had been buried 360 years earlier beneath the floor of All Saints Church in Suffolk, England. However, forensic analysis of the skeleton showed that the unmarked burial contained the remains of another much younger individual (age 45 years). A DNA sample was also sought for Gosnold's niece who was said to be buried at a neighboring church, but the grave was never found.

JAMESTOWN DOUBLE BURIAL
The burial occurred during the summer of 1607. It was found inside the perimeter of James Fort near burials of 34 others. Records from the first year of the colony are limited, but colonist George Percy's accounting of men lost mentions three occasions when pairs of men died on the same day, suggesting that they may have been buried together. Archaeologists have excavated two of these double burials and have located a third "extra-wide" grave nearby. Evidence of steps dug into the ground to reach the burial is visible. Two men had been buried side by side, their heads to the north and touching the grave wall. An extra 24 inches of space extended past their feet, and a low shelf ran along one side of the shaft, as though the diggers were inexperienced and had dug the grave much bigger than necessary. Looking down at the bones, it appeared that both men had been wrapped in shrouds, as their knees were close together and one man's jaw was tightly clenched.

JAMES FORT BOY
In August 2005, a skeleton was discovered during an excavation by archaeologists of APVA Preservation Virginia/Historic Jamestowne inside James Fort along the western palisade wall. An historic written account says that a young Englishman died after an attack by Indians in 1607.

129

NOTES

JAMESTOWN TREPHINATION

A skull fragment found in a James Fort trash pit preserved remarkable medical evidence. Circular cut marks into the bone are the earliest known case in the English colonies of attempted trephination—drilling into the cranium to relieve pressure caused by brain swelling. One impact caused radiating fractures on the lower left side of the skull. Another injury caused a radiating fracture on the right side of the skull. These blows would have caused severe intracranial swelling.

Straight cuts also provide evidence of the earliest known autopsy in the Chesapeake. After the patient died, the top of the cranium was removed for a postmortem examination.

During the autopsy, the deceased was placed face down, and the surgeon sawed through the posterior vault. The cranial fragment found in the trash pit broke away from the rest of the skull along perimortem fracture lines.

JAMESTOWN WELL

Cranium of a teenaged English boy *in situ*, in a James Fort well that had been abandoned and filled with trash (ca.1615). Archaeologists installed wooden wall supports during the 2006 excavation of this Jamestown well to prevent the walls from collapsing. There was exceptional preservation of many artifacts and human remains due to the water and the an-aerobic environment. Where oxygen is scarce, there is little bacterial activity and decay oc-curs slowly. These cranial bones survived deep in the James Fort well. The bone is so well preserved that it looks recent.

THE BRICK CHAPEL, HISTORIC ST. MARY'S CITY, MARYLAND

St. Mary's City, Maryland was settled in March 1634, along the St. Mary's River, a tributary of the Potomac, in what is now Maryland. St. Mary's City is one of the best preserved founding sites of a 17th-century English colony in North America. A foundation in the shape of a Latin cross lay buried for three centuries, an archaeological puzzle piece believed to have been the base of a Catholic church dismantled a little more than three decades after it was built. Scattered clues supported the idea of a lost church: fragments of brick, plaster and glass found at the site, and mention of a "good brick Chappell" in the writings of an early colonial governor.

As part of its interpretive program, Historic St. Mary's City decided to reconstruct the church based on archaeological and historical research. As part of preparing for this project, a corridor five feet wide around the exterior perimeter of the church's foundation was excavated, which exposed more than 60 burials, providing a well-preserved sample of Maryland's early population.

CALVERT LEAD COFFINS

In 1992, archaeologists excavated three lead coffins at the site of the Brick Chapel in St. Mary's City. In the colonial period, burial in lead coffins was a sign of great wealth. At the time of the excavation, the area was still an open field that had been a cornfield for centuries. There was no indication that this was a burial site. The lead coffins were discovered during an archaeological remote sensing survey. The two largest coffins were identified as the remains of Chancellor and Governor Philip Calvert and his wife, Anne Wolseley Calvert. The third coffin contained the remains of an infant. Births, deaths, and marriages were rarely recorded in the colonial Chesapeake. Historical records on infants or children are virtually nonexistent, even for those born to families of high social status. Because Anne Wolseley Calvert was at least 60 years old at her death, this baby could not have been hers. The skeleton pictured above was most likely a child born to Philip Calvert and his second wife, Jane Sewell.

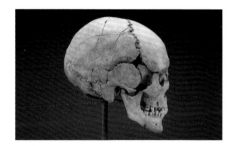

INDENTURED SERVANT BURIAL
LEAVY NECK MARYLAND

Leavy Neck is the name of a colonial property in the settlement of Providence, St. Margaret's County, the first Puritan settlement in Maryland. The Leavy Neck site is located off Mill Creek on St. Margaret's across the Severn River from Annapolis. Archaeologists with the Anne Arundel County's Lost Towns Project dated the deposit that lies over the burial to the mid-1660s.

In November, 2003, the archaeology team discovered the skeleton while excavating the basement of a dwelling on the property. The remains of a 16-year-old male had been stuffed into a corner of a cellar wall. Analysis of his bones showed severe spinal trauma. How a body is treated after death also reveals something about its identity. This disturbing burial shows how little the boy's life was valued. The treatment of indentured servants as if they were mere chattel was so common that a 1663 Maryland law proposed outlawing the private burial of servants. There were fractures in the boy's radius and metacarpal bones as well as the ribs. Since the wounds appear to be defensive, and the burial clandestine, the boy was likely the victim of violence.

CENTREVILLE, VIRGINIA
UNKNOWN CIVIL WAR SOLDIERS

Six young adult Caucasian males were buried while their military unit was encamped in the Centreville area during the Civil War, 1861-1865. The skeletal remains were examined at the National Museum of Natural History (NMNH), Smithsonian Institution. Dental caries and abscessing are the primary disease processes evident in the six individuals. The cause of death could only be determined with certainty for Burial 3 (gunshot wound to the head). Aside from Burials 3 and 6, it seems unlikely that the other men died as a result of trauma sustained in battle, although bone preservation was poor.

131

NOTES

EMMANUEL LUTHERAN CHURCH
UNKNOWN CONFEDERATE SOLDIERS
THE BATTLE OF NEW MARKET, VIRGINIA
In May, 1864, Federal troops moved
southward into the town of New Market,
Virginia. On that rainy day Federal forces
under Major General Franz Sigel were
attacked by Confederate units. The
southern ranks included the cadets of the
Virginia Military Institute. The Rebels were
lead by the charismatic Major General
John C. Breckinridge. Sigel was driven from
the field in rout but with a terrible cost of
lives on both sides.

Local lore indicated that soldiers who had
died during the battle had been buried in a
"soldiers" plot within the church cemetery.
Owsley was asked to determine whether
military burials were present before the
church used the area for new graves. Five
unmarked burials were initially examined
in situ, measured, mapped, and then removed
for transport to the Smithsonian Institution.
Of the five burials, three were identified as
Confederate soldiers and two as civilians.

CONFEDERATE PRIVATE ISAAC NEWTON
MASON 1826-1862
Isaac Newton Mason, born in 1826 in
Pulaski, Tennessee, was a wealthy man for
his times. The 1860 US Census values his
personal property at $23,865 and his real
estate at 1,640 acres, which included
27 persons who were enslaved. The family's
fortune was virtually wiped out during the
Civil War by the pillaging of the Federal
Army and by marauding bands of civilians.
Newton enlisted in the Confederate Army
as a private in the 11th Tennessee Cavalry
Regiment in 1861. He survived the Battle
of Shiloh in April 1862.

Isaac Newton Mason is reported to have
died in April or May 1862 from injuries
incurred from a fall near Luca, Mississippi.
Somehow his body was returned to Giles
County, Tennessee, a rare event since
nearly 800 soldiers from this locality died
during the war and fewer than a dozen were
brought home for burial. It is assumed that
his brother brought him back. No bone
injuries were evident in the forensic analysis;
an elapsed time between death and burial
was indicated. Isaac Newton Mason was
buried with his boots on—custom-made
leather riding boots.

His well-preserved silk necktie shown above.

CONFEDERATE CAPT WM. D. FARLEY
Killed in the Battle of Brandy Station, June
9th, 1863, Captain Wm. D. Farley, South
Carolinian and graduate of the University
of Virginia School of Law, was one of Major
General J.E.B. Stuart's key scouts. The battle
of Brandy Station was the largest cavalry
engagement by the southern horseman.
Farley was mortally wounded while sitting
astride his horse discussing orders with
Colonel Matthew Calbraith Butler. A cannon
ball passed through his horse and severed
his right leg at the knee. While others were
helping Butler, whose foot was blown off by
the same cannonball, Farley asked Lt. John
T. Rhett to bring him his severed leg. Rhett
would later write that Will "pressed it to his
bosom as one would a child," and said, "It is
an old friend, gentlemen, and I do not wish
to part from it." A shadow of black dirt in
the red clay showed the captain lying with
his left leg intact but his right one cut off at
the knee. The imprint of his severed limb
was clearly visible, resting close beside the
left leg.

On October 21, 2001, after 138 years,
Confederate Captain William Downs Farley
was finally granted his wish. His remains,
buried in the plot of a Culpeper, Virginia,
family, were finally going home to Laurens,
South Carolina.

Field foreman, Rich Richardson (above), also
worked on the Centreville site.

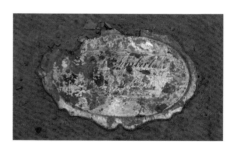

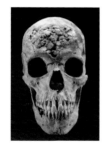

A.B. TIMBERLAKE IRON COFFIN
HANOVER COUNTY, VIRGINIA
The story begins in June 1862, as Union troops under Gen. George McClellan pushed their way toward Richmond. Union soldiers rounded up Timberlake with about 100 other Virginia farmers and took them to a prison camp. In poor health before he was captured, Timberlake never recovered after he was released three weeks later. He died at his brother's home in Richmond and his body was brought back to his plantation for burial in the family cemetery.

More than 140 years after A.B. Timberlake was buried, his body made its way to the Smithsonian laboratory. Once the rusted bolts were sawed through and lead seal chiseled open, six men hoisted the 125-pound lid from the iron coffin to reveal the mortal remains of Archibald Burnett Timberlake. A silver plate (above) on the coffin's lid said simply, "A.B. Timberlake, age 53 years." He was dressed in a black cutaway jacket with velvet lapels. Scattered bits of a beard littered the remains of a silk cravat. One of the first things that was noted as a possible cause of death was a severe tooth abscess. However, osteological analysis revealed severe deformation of the vertebrae characteristic of advanced tuberculosis.

AFRICAN LIVES IN AMERICA
A CASE OF MISTAKEN IDENTITY
First Identified as Native American in the 1940s, re-examination by Smithsonian anthropologists showed that four skeletons found at Colonial Jamestown are among the oldest known remains of Africans in America. The bones were thought to date between 1650 and 1675. One of the Jamestown skeletons, that of a man in his mid-20s (pictured above), is riddled with pits and deformations typical of end-stage syphilis. The man must have been in great pain and suffering from severe dementia. The skull shows that the man died of a gunshot wound to the head, possibly the result of a mercy killing.

The X-ray on page 4, reveals a gunshot wound and radiating fractures. The visible white specks evident in this radiograph are tiny fragments of metal that splintered off the lead ball.

RUTLAND SLAVE CEMETERY HANOVER COUNTY, VA
Hanover County is located in the Richmond-Petersburg region and is part of the Richmond Metropolitan Statistical Area. The remains of 57 enslaved people of African descent were found in an unmarked cemetery on the Timberlake property known as the Rutland Plantation. When the cemetery was located, Smithsonian scientists along with local scientists and scholars were asked to oversee extensive research and analysis of the remains. As a result of this historical and scientific work, a group of individuals who had not been heard in life, were finally given a voice.

The first known Africans in the Chesapeake arrived in 1619. Taken from a Portuguese slave ship by English privateers, some 20 to 30 men and women from Angola were brought to Virginia as servants or slaves. There is some reference to Africans in court cases and a very few individuals of African ancestry were mentioned as "free-man" who owned property. In the early 1600s it was possible for people of African ancestry to gain their freedom or arrive in the colonies as free men. Circumstances changed in the mid-1600s when plantation owners began turning to race-based slavery for labor and profit.

NOTES

HARLEIGH KNOLL SITE
TALBOT COUNTY, MARYLAND
Harleigh Knoll is a wetlands area in the Talbot County tidal flats on Maryland's Eastern Shore. Its distinguishing feature is a mound of earth, less than 9 feet of sandy soil. It looked like a typical 17th-century–European cemetery with small boulders used as tombstones, east-west orientation of the bodies, and hexagonal "toe pincher" coffins. The field work began in October 2004. At least 34 individuals were found buried at the site, most in a formal, orderly manner. Upon examination, it was learned that some remains were of European and others of African descent. It is possible that the cemetery dated from the earliest days of slavery (1730–1770) when poor and powerless people, whether enslaved or indentured, were commonly buried together. The records suggest as few as 300 African people were living on the Eastern Shore in 1665.

The Harleigh Knoll site was excavated by a crew of experienced archaeologists who volunteered their time, including two experts in the use of ground-penetrating radar (GPR). A group of students and teachers from three Eastern Shore high schools were invited to join the team.

FACIAL RECONSTRUCTION METHODS
Over the last 100 years, there have been various methods used to produce reconstructions for forensic identification as well as for historical or archaeological purposes. Making a facial reconstruction is an exacting and expensive process. Using tissue depth standards taken from hundreds of people, it is possible to rebuild, in clay, what a person's face might have looked like during life. These steps require a trained sculptor familiar with facial anatomy working together with a forensic anthropologist who can interpret skeletal features.

WWII BLEIBURG MASSACRE
In May of 1945, near the end of World War II, close to the village of Bleiburg on the Austrian-Slovenian border, some 30,000 POWs, surrendered personnel, and refugees, along with another 60,000 soldiers and civilians fleeing from the defeated independent State of Croatia, were hoping to surrender to the Allies. When they reached the British 5th Corps Headquarters on the Austrian border, they were all forcibly turned back.

Thousands were captured and massacred by the communist Yugoslav partisan army under its Supreme Commander, Josip Tito. Many had their hands wired behind their backs and were shot in the back of the head before open pits. The atrocities were said to be a reprisal for suspected collaboration with the Wehrmacht or the Ustashe party. Owsley and team worked on 98 individuals whose remains were recovered from one of four mass graves in the fields near Bleiburg. The bagged remains pictured on page 97 were recovered by civilians who didn't want the massacre to be forgotten or denied.

HOMELAND WAR, GLINA, CROATIA

In 1996-1997 Douglas Owsley made several trips to Zagreb as part of a joint Croatian-US forensic investigative team to teach doctors the techniques and instrumentation employed in the discovery, excavation, and examination of human remains. The team's objective was to help identify victims of mass killings and murders in the region around Glina, Croatia during the 1991-95 Serbian conflicts. The Croatian team was led by forensic pathologist Dr. Davor Strinović (Department of Forensic Medicine at the School of Medicine, University of Zagreb) and by Mario Šlaus of the Zavod du Arheologiju, University of Zagreb. Šlaus had studied under Owsley as an intern with the Smithsonian's Fellowship Program.

Besides identifying the deceased and determining the cause of death, the forensic team also recorded cranial and postcranial skeletal measurements for an osteometric data bank being developed for the region. Such information would aid future personal identifications by providing important comparative data. The identification and proper reburial of the missing dead and the international community's participation in this effort was an essential part of the peace and reconstruction process.

VLADIMIR DEVIDÉ

Spaljeno selo.
Pas lutalica njuši
pougljene kosti.

In the burned-out village
a wounded stray dog
sniffing charred bones

This haiku is related to tragic events of the 1990s. It serves as an example of the aggression on Croatia, and was written in 1991 by Professor Devidé. Born in 1925, Zagreb, Croatia, Devidé is professor emeritus in mathematics at the University of Zagreb.

Bart Mesotten, English translation, Duizend Kolibries (A Thousand Hummingbirds, Flemish Edition) Belgium, 1993.

WACO TRAGEDY

The Waco siege began on February 28, 1993, when the US Bureau of Alcohol, Tobacco, and Firearms attempted to serve a search warrant at the Branch Davidian ranch near Waco, Texas. An exchange of gunfire resulted in the deaths of four agents and six Davidians. A subsequent 51-day siege by the FBI ended on April 19, when fire destroyed the compound. Eighty people, including children, died in the fire along with Davidian leader Vernon Wayne Howell, a.k.a. David Koresh. The complexity of the case required the formation of a large multidisciplinary forensics team. The contributions of the Smithsonian anthropologists were of two major types: the recovery of human remains from the site and the analysis of human remains. The anthropology team re-assembled Koresh's fragmented skull. A bullet had entered the center of his forehead and exited in the occipital area. This head wound, fired at close range, was determined to be the cause of Koresh's death.

135

NOTES

SKELETAL DONATED COLLECTIONS

THE ROBERT J. TERRY ANATOMICAL SKELETAL COLLECTION, NATIONAL MUSEUM OF NATURAL HISTORY, SMITHSONIAN INSTITUTION

A collection of human skeletons is held by the Department of Anthropology of the National Museum of Natural History, Smithsonian Institution. It was created by Robert J. Terry (1871-1966) during his time as professor of anatomy and head of the Anatomy Department at Washington University Medical School in St. Louis, Missouri from 1899 until his retirement in 1941. It was transferred to its present holders in 1967. The collection is an invaluable source for anthropological research because of the extensive documentation that accompanies each skeleton. The Terry Collection presently consists of 1,728 individuals of known age, sex, ancestry, cause of death and pathological conditions. File records contain individual morgue records, anthropometric measurements, dental charts, bone inventories and autopsy reports. Associated photographs, plaster death masks and hair samples are correlated by file number.

WILLIAM M. BASS DONATED SKELETAL COLLECTION, FORENSIC ANTHROPOLOGY CENTER, UNIVERSITY OF TENNESSEE, KNOXVILLE

William Bass founded the Tennessee Forensic Anthropology Center, the world's first major scientific facility devoted to studying human decomposition, better known as the "body farm." Donated remains make this research possible and simultaneously provide a modern osteological teaching collection. Presently, this demographically rich collection consists of almost 400 skeletons, essential for providing education and training in forensic anthropology and skeletal biology for students and law enforcement agencies. They are also invaluable for updating demographic and biological standards. The goal of the body donation program is to build this collection of known individuals for research purposes. Owsley was trained in forensic methodology by William Bass during his graduate career at the University of Tennessee where he received his Masters in 1975 and his PhD in 1978. Owsley describes Bass as an inspiration and a lifelong mentor.

FORENSIC ANTHROPOLOGY DATA BANK

The FDB was initiated by Dr. Richard Jantz at the Department of Anthropology of the University of Tennessee, Knoxville, as a way to obtain contemporary osteometric data of sex, ancestry, and age from modern individuals. Prior to 1986, forensic identification criteria were based almost exclusively on the large anatomical collections (Terry and Hamann-Todd) containing individuals with mainly 19th century birth dates.

The FDB has nearly 2,900 cases. Sex and ancestry has been confirmed in over 1,800 cases. Of these, 1,731 are positively identified individuals. Many of these individuals have been measured and submitted by forensic anthropologists around the country. J. Lawrence Angel, curator of the Smithsonian Department of Anthropology from 1962-1986, analyzed 400 cases over a period of 25 years. These make up one of the largest components of the database.

Bone measurements indicate that the American population has changed. Skeletal change in stature and physical size presumably results from the unparalleled environmental changes that have occurred over the past 100 years. They include better nutrition and health and fewer mechanical demands on the skeleton. In addition the composition of the American population continues to change with immigration and different rates of natural increase. The Forensic Anthropology Data Bank provides the opportunity to monitor these skeletal changes as they occur.

left to right
Chip Clark
John Imlay

left to right
Laurie Burgess
Douglas Owsley
Karin Bruwelhcide

left to right
Aleithea Williams
Cass Taylor

left to right
Karin Bruwelheide
Vicki Simon
Dana Kollmann

left to right
Bill Hanna
Dale Brown
Rich Richardson (4 July, 1929 - 15 December, 2006)

SOURCE CREDITS

Byers, Steven N. and Susan M.T. Myster. 2005 *Forensic Anthropology Laboratory Manual*. Pearson Education Inc.

Bruwelheide, K.S., J. Beck and S. Pelot. 2001. Standardized protocol for radiographic and photographic documentation of human skeletons. In *Human Remains: Conservation, Retrieval and Analysis*. BAR International Series. 153-166.

Buikstra J.E. and D.H. Ubelaker. 1994. Standards for data collection from human skeletal remains. *Arkansas Archeological Survey Research* Series 44.

Moore, L.E., D.W. Owsley and K.L. Sandness [Bruwelheide]. 1995. Military and civilian burials from Centreville, Virginia. *Quarterly Bulletin of the Archaeological Society* of Virginia 50(4): 27-45.

Owsley, D.W. and B.E. Compton. 1990. The Smithsonian Anthropology Collections: planning for long-term use. *Museum Anthropology* 14(3): 11-15.

Owsley, D.W. 1992. The what, why, and how of forensic anthropology, in *Discovering Anthropology*, Daniel R. Gross, Mayfield Publishing, 189-199.

Owsley, D.W. 1995. Techniques for locating burials, with emphasis on the probe. *Journal of Forensic Sciences* 40(5): 735-740.

Owsley, D.W., D.H. Ubelaker, M.M. Houck, K. L. Sandness [Bruwelheide], W.E. Grant, E.A. Craig, T.J. Woltanski and N. Peerwani. 1995. The role of forensic anthropology in the recovery and analysis of Branch Davidian compound victims: techniques of analysis. *Journal of Forensic Sciences* 40 (3): 341-348.

Owsley, D.W. 1996. Forensic anthropology and bioarchaeology at the Smithsonian Institution, *CRM Journal* 19 (10): 21-25.

Owsley, D.W., Davor Strinović, Mario Šlaus, Dana D. Kollmann and Malcolm Richardson. 1996. Recovery and identification of civilian victims of war in Croatia. *CRM Journal*, 19(10): 33-36.

Owsley, D.W., K. Bruwelheide, and R. Kardash. 2001. Recovery and analysis of the Jamestown Rediscovery south churchyard burials from the 1999 field season. *Journal of the Jamestown Rediscovery Center* No.1.

Owsley, D.W. 2001. Why the forensic anthropologist needs the archaeologist. *Historical Archaeology*, 35(1): 35-38.

Owsley, D.W., W.F. Hanna, M.L. Richardson, and L.E. Burgess. 2002 Bioarchaeological and geophysical investigation, the soldiers plot, Emmanuel Lutheran Church Cemetery, New Market, Virginia. *Archaeological Society of Virginia Special Publication*, 41, Spectrum Press: 1-60.

Owsley, D.W., M.L. Richardson, and C.K. Gailey III. 2002. Military service identification of soldiers buried in a church cemetery in New Market, Virginia. *ASV Quarterly Bulletin* 57(4): 218-220.

Owsley, D.W., M.L.Richardson, and W.F. Hanna. 2003. Bioarchaeological investigation of the grave of William D Farley, Confederate Scout. *Quarterly Bulletin of the Archaeological Society of Virginia* 58(2): 94-113.

Owsley, D.W. 2006. Kennewick Man detailed. 2007. *Science Year*. World Book Inc. 165-166.

Owsley, D.W., K.S. Bruwelheide, L.W. Cartmell, Sr., Laurie E. Burgess, Shelley J.Foote, Skye M. Chang, and Nick Fielder. 2006. The man in the iron coffin: an interdisciplinary effort to name the past. *Historical Archaeology* 40(3): 89-108.

Unpublished Manuscripts

Owsley, D.W., K.S. Bruwelheide, M. Cashion Lugo, and J.-L. Romero Palanco. Forensic identification of Ramón Power Y Giralt: Puerto Rico's diplomat to the 1812 Spanish Constitutional Court.

Owsley, D.W., K.S. Bruwelheide, and S.K. Reidy. The Lee Family tomb at Darnall's Chance, Upper Marlboro, Maryland.

Owsley, D.W. and B. E. Compton. 1992. An osteological investigation of human remains from Jordan's Journey (Site 44PG302), a 17th-century fortified settlement in Prince George County, Virginia. Virginia Department of Historic Resources, Richmond.

POETRY CREDITS

p.10 Wright, Charles. "Body Language." *Negative Blue*, Farrar, Straus & Giroux, 2001.

p.25 Reprinted by permission of the publishers and the Trustees of Amherst College from THE POEMS OF EMILY DICKENSON: READING EDITION, edited by Ralph W. Franklin, Cambridge, Mass.: The Belknap Press of Harvard University Press, Copyright: ©1998, 1999 by the President and Fellows of Harvard College. Copyright ©1951, 1955, 1979, 1983 by the President and Fellows of Harvard College Company, 1976.

p.26 Johnson, Georgia Douglas. "Common Dust." *Anthology of Modern American Poetry*. Ed. Cary Nelson. Oxford University Press, 2000.

p.38 Logue, Christopher. "War Music." *War Music: An Account of Books 1-4 and 16-19 of Homer's Iliad.* Farrar Straus & Giroux, 1997.

p.71 Lowell, Robert. "For the Union Dead." *Life Studies and For the Union Dead* Noonday Press, Farrar, Straus & Giroux, Inc., 1964.

p.90 Evans, Mari. "I Am a Black Woman." *Continuum: New and Selected Poems,* Black Classic Press, 2007.

p.103 Devidé, Vladimir. "In the burned-out village." Bart Mesotten, translator. Haiku, Duizend Kolibries (A Thousand Hummingbirds, Flemish Edition), Belgium, 1993. Copyright © 2001 World Haiku Association.

p.126 Arthur, Robert P. *Hymn to the Chesapeake,* Road Publishers, 1996.

TEXT CREDITS

p.72 Quote, Sam Watkins, *Company Aytch: or A Side Show of the Big Show.* Plume, 1999. Originally published, 1882.

p.95 Quote, Greg Palazzolo, Palazzolo *Design, in the Art of Design*, HOW Design Books, 2003.

p.98 Arendt, Hannah. *The Origins of Totalitarianism*, New York, Harcourt, 1951.

p.107 Quote, Michel Certeau, from *The Practice of Everyday Life*. Translated by Steven Rendall. University of California Press. 1984.

NOTES Based in part on Written in Bone exhibition script by MFMDesign/VossWords.

SCULPTURE CREDITS

pp.40, 41, 49, 59, 61, 93, 129 Sculpted busts by StudioEIS.

PHOTOGRAPHY CREDITS

Smithsonian Senior Science Photographer: Chip Clark

Photography Exceptions:
Cover, pp. 59, 64, 89, 114, 115, 116
Brittney Tatchell, Smithsonian Physical Anthropology Intern

p.92 Donald E. Hurlbert, Staff Photographer National Museum of Natural History

p.96 Dana Kollmann, Baltimore County Police Department, Forensic Services Technician

p.118 Vicky Karas and Mel Wachowiak Smithsonian Museum Conservation Institute

p.118 Historic St. Mary's City, CT scan of fiber

pp.8, 10, 93 © 2008 Kate Meyers

WEB

APVA Preservation Virginia:
http://www.apva.org/Historic

St. Mary's City Museum:
http://www.stmaryscity.org/

Smithsonian Anthro Notes:
http://anthropology.si.edu/outreach/anthnote/anthronotes.html

University of Tennessee:
http://web.utk.edu/~fac/

CREDITS

INDEX

INDEX